FACES OF THE CENTURY
A SAINSBURY'S PHOTOGRAPHIC EXHIBITION

Wyggeston and Queen

Pleas

FACES OF THE CENTURY

A SAINSBURY'S PHOTOGRAPHIC EXHIBITION

NATIONAL PORTRAIT GALLERY

Published to accompany the exhibition *Faces of the Century* held at the
National Portrait Gallery, London, from 22 October 1999 to 30 January 2000

Sponsored by **Sainsbury's**

Published in Great Britain by National Portrait Gallery Publications,
National Portrait Gallery, St Martin's Place, London WC2H 0HE

ISBN 1 85514 274 0

A catalogue record for this book is available from the British Library.

Senior Editor: *Lucy Clark*
Project Manager: *Delia Gaze*
Designer: *Richard Adams Associates*
Printed by *EBS, Italy*

For a complete catalogue of current publications, please write to the address above.

Frontispiece:
Beatlemania, 26 October 1965. Central Press/Hulton Getty (detail of page 156).

Contents

Acknowledgements

The Gallery wishes to thank the following for their assistance:

Natasha Alderslade; Murray Blewitt; Lesley Jane Bradshaw; Andrew Brooke; Kate Chertavian; Helen Coyle; Eileen d'Arcy; Glazer Design Associates; Lennie Goodings; Hilary Hard; Michael Hoppen; Valerie Kemp; Virginia Lohte; Lady Deborah Macmillan; Dadu Patel; Amit Roy; Frances Topp; Ros Wall; Brett Rogers and Sean Williams of the British Council; Erica Davies of the Freud Museum; Em Parkinson and Colin Finlay of the Hulton Getty Picture Collection; Phil Dunn of the National Museum of Labour History; Honor Clerk, Antonia Leak and Miriam Perez of the National Portrait Gallery; Francesca Franchi of the Royal Opera House; James Holloway and Sara Stevenson of the Scottish National Portrait Gallery; Sarah Woodcock of the Theatre Museum.

The Selectors' Brief

The selectors were asked to bear in mind the following criteria when selecting images to represent the century:

Photographs of impressive quality that for the individual selector represent an aspect of British life in the twentieth century that is worthy of remembrance. They should be photographs of people famous or unknown, individually or in groups.

Preface

EARLY IN 1997, Lord Sainsbury approached the National Portrait Gallery with an idea which had arisen at one of the meetings of Sainsbury's Arts Sponsorship panel, which he chairs. The company supports a wide range of arts initiatives on an annual basis. It had been suggested that in 1999 the company should sponsor an exhibition which would mark the new millennium by looking back on the last 100 years, with a display of 100 photographs to be described as *Faces of the Century*. Sainsbury's hoped that it would be possible to organise this exhibition in collaboration with the National Portrait Gallery.

The idea of representing British history through portraiture has been close to the heart of the National Portrait Gallery ever since its foundation in 1856. Since the late 1960s, we have been increasingly involved in collecting photographic portraits, a side of the Gallery's activity that is less well known than its primary collection of paintings, sculpture and drawings. As we were already thinking about ideas for celebrating the end of the century, the idea of working with Sainsbury's was inevitably appealing. It would be a way of giving the exhibition a mass audience which the Gallery would like to reach, as well as the funding to make the exhibition possible.

From the beginning of the project, there were three fixed points to it. The first was the title of the exhibition — *Faces of the Century: A Sainsbury's Photographic Exhibition* — which describes its content. The second was the briefing statement drafted by Sainsbury's Arts Sponsorship panel and used by the Gallery to guide selectors in their choices. The third was the idea that there should be diversity in the choice of selectors in order to give different views of what was important in the century, rather than a monolithic narrative.

The third aspect of the exhibition — the idea that it should exhibit diversity in its account of the century's history — is perhaps the most important. The exhibition is not intended to add up to a uniform and consistent account of the history of the century. There are inevitably omissions, as well as unexpected inclusions. This is because the exhibition is about how different people think about the past. It is about unorthodox and personal views of history. It is a game which anyone can play. And I hope that disagreement with what the selectors have chosen will prompt visitors to the exhibition to think about what their version of the country's century might be.

Lord Sainsbury has undoubtedly been a driving force behind the exhibition. He has organised a schedule of meetings, kept us up to the mark, and taken great pains to ensure that his own selection sets the highest possible standard for others to follow. Next, we would both wish to thank the selectors, who have taken up the challenge in exactly the spirit they were intended to, with careful thought about how to shape their view of history with an exiguous palette of only ten photographs each. Then, I hope that the selectors would agree that an essential key to the project has been the encyclopaedic knowledge of Terence Pepper, the Gallery's curator of photography. He is the person who has been able to translate the suggestions of selectors, who may have come with the vaguely remembered image of a particular photograph they might wish to include, into the reality of an exhibition. Alongside Terence Pepper, Kathleen Soriano, the Gallery's Head of Exhibitions and Collections Management, has, even more than usual, made the exhibition happen, keeping a close eye on all the logistical arrangements and coming in from maternity leave in order to ensure that everything was running as smoothly as possible. Beyond these people lie many others: the team at Sainsbury's, particularly Marah Winn Moon and Fiona Matthews; the Hulton Getty Picture Collection, who have generously given support towards the many images chosen from their collection; Martha Brookes of the Exhibitions department at the National Portrait Gallery; Susan Bright of the Photography department; the Gallery's PR and Development department, particularly Pim Baxter, Ben Rawlingson Plant and Emma Marlow; and the Gallery's Publications department, who have produced a catalogue which will be a long-lasting record of the exhibition. Roger Hargreaves of the Education department has produced a schools' resource pack and organised a series of workshops and lectures. But most of all, we are grateful to Sainsbury's for their generous and creative sponsorship.

Charles Saumarez Smith
Director

Sponsor's Foreword

AS CHAIRMAN of the Sainsbury's Art Sponsorship Panel, I am delighted that we are the originators and the sponsors of *Faces of the Century*, an exhibition intended to mark the new millennium. That it has been possible is due to the National Portrait Gallery and to the enthusiasm and support of the Director, Charles Saumarez Smith, and his staff. They have, with considerable expertise and knowledge, organised the exhibition and assisted the ten selectors by sourcing those photographs from the Gallery's archives and other collections that best reflected their wishes. For us all it has been a most happy co-operation. Particular thanks should go to Terence Pepper, whose exhaustive knowledge we all found invaluable, and to all his colleagues, who have contributed so much to the exhibition.

We are fortunate in having such a distinguished and diverse group of selectors bringing contrasting approaches to the choice of *Faces of the Century*, which I believe adds considerably to the interest of the exhibition. I am extremely grateful to them all for giving the task so much thought and originality, as well as their most valuable time. As a somewhat reluctant one of the ten, I found it much harder to choose ten 'Faces' than I believe it would have been to choose one hundred.

Let me add how pleased we are to be supporting the extensive educational programme that has been organised by the Gallery. This will allow a considerable number of school visits both here and in the other venues of the exhibition. These I am happy to say are to be in Hull, Bath and Stirling during 2000.

Finally I hope that you find the exhibition enjoyable, informative, stimulating and timely. May it cause some reflection on the personalities and events of the past 100 years as we move into the 21st century.

John Sainsbury

Sainsbury's Programme of Arts Sponsorship

SAINSBURY'S ARTS Sponsorship programme, which was established in 1981, has won many awards for excellence. The programme is designed to deliver high quality, imaginative and dynamic arts sponsorships involving as many people as possible in the communities where we trade. We create our own unique Sainsbury's schemes as well as lending support to particular regional and local projects.

Sainsbury's Pictures for Schools involves giving framed reproductions of great paintings to schools across the country. We aim to bring art to young people in a familiar environment, in the hope that we will encourage an enthusiasm for pictures and an interest in visiting art galleries. Our emphasis is on achieving reproductions of the highest standard and the scheme attracts very positive feedback from children, teachers and parents. Over 7000 primary, secondary and special needs schools have benefited. In 2000 we are planning to give another 1000 primary schools a set of four pictures; the selector for the 2000 scheme is Sir Nicholas Serota, Director of the Tate Gallery.

Sainsbury's Choir of the Year is a biennial competition open to amateur choirs across the UK. Over 10,000 singers in some 300 choirs enter the competition, which is televised by the BBC in a series of programmes over the Christmas holiday and watched by more than 1 million people.

In 2000 the final of the competition will be held at the Royal Albert Hall. It is intended to be a glorious celebration of all that is good in British choral singing with showcase performances from the best amateur choirs in the country plus a massed ensemble piece involving both choirs and audience.

Sainsbury's Youth Orchestra Series provides concert sponsorship for selected orchestras enabling them to engage professional conductors and soloists or book prestigious venues. Up to six of the concerts are then broadcast by Classic FM. Since the series was launched nearly one hundred concerts have been supported.

Support both of choirs and of youth orchestras makes Sainsbury's one of the country's largest sponsors of young amateur music-making.

Sainsbury's Checkout Theatre encourages and promotes new quality theatre at low prices for young people and their families. Over the next three years, Sainsbury's will be commissioning new plays for this audience and will be working with theatres and Sainsbury's stores across the country to attract the next generation of theatregoers.

Local and regional projects
Alongside these specially created sponsorships, we also support a number of regional and local projects. We take account of the geographical and artform spread and our local managers are closely involved both in the selection of the initiatives and in their development to provide creative links with our stores.

DAVID BOWIE

BORN IN Brixton, London, in 1947, the rock singer, songwriter and actor David Bowie began his career at the age of 16, releasing his first hit single, 'Space Oddity', in 1969. His albums include *Ziggy Stardust* (1972), *Diamond Dogs* (1974), *Stage* (1978), *Scary Monsters* (1980), *Let's Dance* (1983), *Outside* (1994) and *Earthling* (1997). He has also acted in films, notably *The Man Who Fell to Earth* (1976), *Just a Gigolo* (1978), *The Hunger* (1982), *Merry Christmas, Mr Lawrence* (1983), *Absolute Beginners* (1986), *The Linguini Incident* (1991) and *Basquiat* (1996), and on the Broadway stage, in *The Elephant Man* (1980). Over the course of his career he has repeatedly recreated his image, changing both the style of his singing and his persona. He is the recipient of numerous international music and entertainment awards.

David Bowie wrote his captions by running each of his titles for his introduction and images through www.AnagramGenius.com, an anagrammatic translator program on the Internet. He then made his choice from the anagrams created to form the text shown here.

Anagrams for the National Portrait Gallery, created using

www.AnagramGenius.com

SEDUCTIVE, FINER cowboy fatheads. Whereabouts scoff tidy deviance. Whereabouts scoffed deviancy it. Seductive, finer fathead cowboys. Twits coffeehouse drab deviancy. Wanted seductive if arch-foe yobs. Show best if favourite decadency. Worst envy efficacious deathbed. Deviance without beady scoffers. Bawdiest deviancy cut-off heroes. Fancy! Bawdiest, seductive of hero. Off deviances abused to witchery. Beauty! witch over-fed of acidness. Sweet deviancy if arch-foe doubts.

DAVID BOWIE

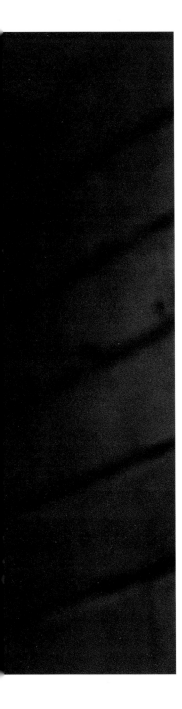

Samuel Beckett Irish playwright
THIS HUGE typewriter blackmails.
Superbly hit witchlike megastar.
Witchlike but slithery rampages.
Pathetic swearers bulk mightily.
Witchlike brute as ghastly prime.
Witchlike guy blasphemer artist.
Witchlike brute graphs steamily.

A novelist, poet and dramatist who wrote in both French and English, Samuel Beckett explored themes of isolation, anguish and the futility of human existence, as in the plays *Waiting for Godot* (1952; English version 1954) and *Not I* (1973).

Samuel Beckett (1906–89)
Jane Bown, 1976
Bromide print,
335 x 493mm
National Portrait Gallery,
London (P373)

DAVID BOWIE

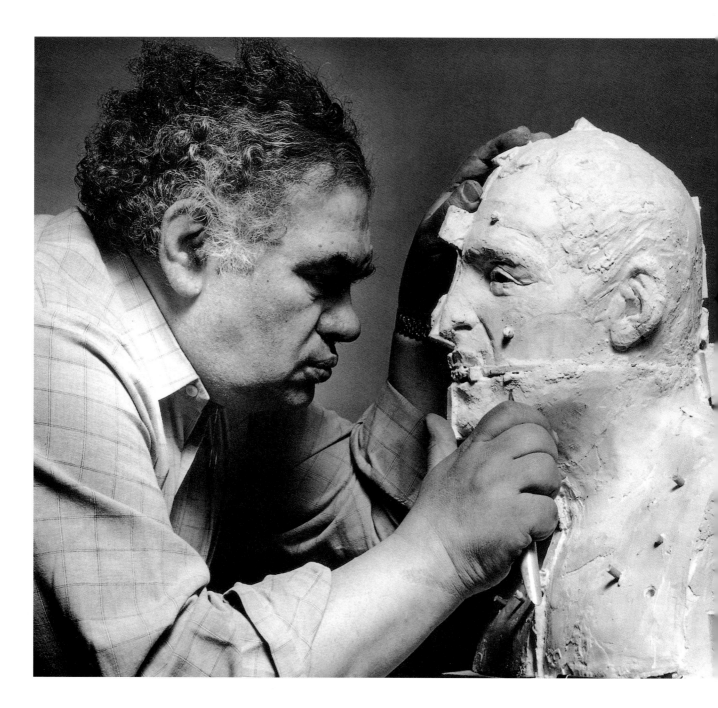

Sir Eduardo Paolozzi British sculptor
STABILIZED RAZOR-SHARP. Razor-sharp
libido dazes riotous it. Is a riotous
traitors drizzled phobia. Battiest or
sordid or hilarious pizza. Blast It!
It is a drizzles abhor odious portrait.

Throughout his career,
working mainly in bronze
and wood, Paolozzi has
been concerned with the
relationship of
technology to art and
society. He was involved
with Pop art, when he
developed an interest in
colour. He has also
experimented with
printmaking.

Eduardo Paolozzi (born
1924) working on his
sculpture of the architect
Richard Rogers.
Frank Thurston, 1988
Toned bromide print,
293 x 392mm
National Portrait Gallery,
London

DAVID BOWIE

McDonald Hobley talking head

AN ODDBALL, cheeky, mad enigma. OK
bellyached and mad loathing. Might
canoodle lanky baldhead. Good!
Backhandedly lethal main. Ole!
Backhandedly mad loathing.

One of the earliest
television personalities,
Hobley joined the BBC
in 1946 after war service
and a career as an actor.
He presented *Talking
Heads* and the magazine
programme *Kaleidoscope*.

McDonald Hobley
(1917–87)
Charles Hewitt,
1 June 1946
Picture Post/
Hulton Getty

John Logie Baird Scottish television inventor

JOVIAL, BRAINIEST, nice smoother despites. Sophisticate major love bite in direness. Objectives or handiest neo-imperialists. An objective smoother responsibilities. It is objective, handsomer personalities.

An electrical engineer, Baird first succeeded in transmitting images by wireless waves in 1924. The BBC tested his system but did not adopt it. He later produced three-dimensional and colour images.

John Logie Baird (1888–1946) watching a test transmission at Radiolympia, London. Stephenson, 31 August 1938 Topical Press/ Hulton Getty

DAVID BOWIE

Peter Lanyon British artist

PRETTILY, IS abhorrent saint? Stealthy or brainiest print. Brainiest trash on prettily. Printers hotter insatiably. It is not this aberrant reply. Abhorrently nastiest rip it. Prettier saint brains hotly. Slithery, aberrant it points.

A landscape painter based in Cornwall, Lanyon was influenced by Ben Nicholson, Naum Gabo and Barbara Hepworth. His paintings show a strong tendency towards abstraction, and his later works reflect his experience of gliding, which he took up in 1959.

From left to right: Patrick Heron (1920–99), Peter Lanyon (1918–64) and Jack Smith (born 1928), Tinner's Arms, Zennor, Cornwall. James Scott, August 1956 Vintage print, 83 x 132mm Sheila Lanyon

DAVID BOWIE

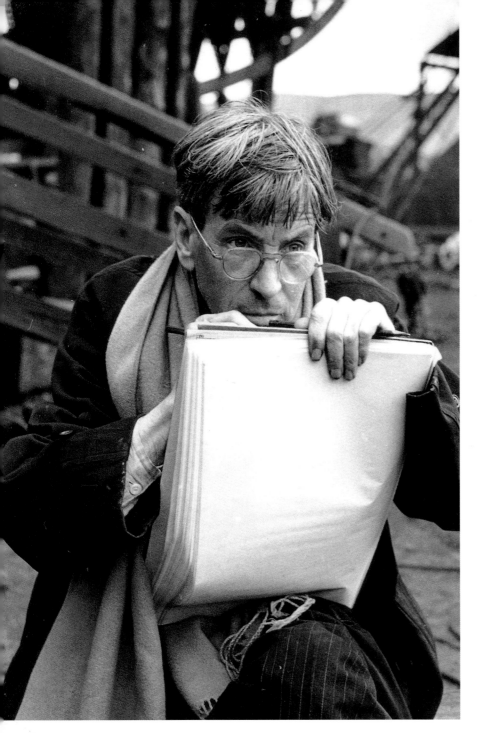

Stanley Spencer British artist
BLAST IT! His tyrannic pesterers. Blast
It! Creep irritant shyness. Sinister rich
patterns beastly. Pretty, brainless,
nastiest rich. Pest brains trashily
intersect. Stealthy instinct raspberries.
Persistently his scatterbrain. Sharp
antics better sinisterly.

Spencer first became
known for pictures that
reflected his experiences
of the First World War.
His visionary works of
the 1920s often have
religious themes, but in
contemporary settings.
He also painted
naturalistic landscapes
and self-portraits.

Stanley Spencer
(1891–1959), sketching
in a Clydeside dockyard.
Leonard McCombe,
2 October 1943
Picture Post/
Hulton Getty

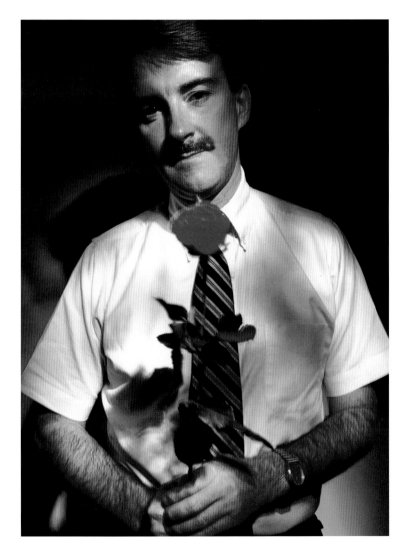

Peter Mandelson British politician
THE BRAINIEST implication splendor.
Bold, happiest, merriest inclination.
Anticipated in horrible simpletons.
Perceptible or nihilist damnations.
Brain nihilism deplores to pittance.
Cheerio! Brilliant disappointments.

Mandelson was an
influential figure in
the formation of 'New
Labour' and in the
election campaign that
led to Tony Blair's victory
in 1997. First Minister
Without Portfolio, then
Secretary of State for
Trade and Industry, he
resigned from the
Cabinet in 1998.

Peter Mandelson
(born 1953)
Steve Speller,
8 August 1988
Cibachrome print,
392 × 291mm
National Portrait Gallery,
London (x34604)

DAVID BOWIE

Sid Vicious punk rock star
RANCID UP kicks virtuosos. Virtuous
sicks and so pricks. Picks so crap
virtuous kind. Carnivorous, stupid
kicks. Pardon! Virtuous, sick. Virtuous
sick on sad prick. Virtuous sick kids on
crap. Productions kick as virus.
Virtuosos crack in up kids.

Vicious joined the punk
group the Sex Pistols in
1977, his leather-clad,
'doomed youth' persona
compensating for his lack
of musical skills. Charged
with the murder of his
girlfriend Nancy Spungen,
he died of a heroin
overdose while out
on bail.

Sid Vicious, I'm a Mess
Sid Vicious (John Simon
Ritchie; 1957–79)
San Antonio, Texas
Bob Gruen, 1978
Cibachrome print,
433 x 330 mm
National Portrait Gallery,
London

DAVID BOWIE

27

A comic entertainer and actor, Wall introduced his most famous character, the grotesque pianist Professor Wallofski, in 1946. His career declined in the 1950s, but later revived, and he enjoyed great success with his one-man show *Aspects of Max Wall* in 1975.

Max Wall (1908–90)
as Professor Wallofski
Unknown photographer
Vintage print,
200 x 250mm
The Raymond Mander
and Joe Mitchenson
Theatre Collection

Max Wall British comedian
HE IS warm, bold anti-climax. Now charitable, dismal mix. His raw, mild exclamation. Cow datable Marx nihilism. Not mixable, wild charisma. A bolder anti-climax whims.

DAVID BOWIE

Peter Cook British comedian
OK! CHAMPION breed eroticist. OK!
Decrepit crab in smoothie. Incorporate
thick embodies. Top-rank, choice,
tiresome bid. Champion restricted
bookie. Crook beat hedonistic prime.
OK aborted in choicest prime.

Cook and his fellow
comedian Dudley Moore
rose to fame in the 1960s
with their satirical
comedy revue *Beyond
the Fringe*, which was
followed by the
celebrated television
series *Not Only . . . But
Also*. He also appeared
in films, and wrote plays
and screenplays.

Peter Cook (1937 95)
Snowdon, 1968

ASA BRIGGS

BORN IN 1921, Asa Briggs read history at Sidney Sussex College, Cambridge. During the Second World War he served in the Intelligence Corps as a cryptographer at Bletchley. He was subsequently Fellow of Worcester College, Oxford (1945–55); Reader in Recent Social and Economic History at Oxford University (1950–55); Professor of Modern History at the University of Leeds (1955–61); and Professor of History at the University of Sussex (1961–76), where he became Vice-Chancellor in 1967. He was Provost of Worcester College, Oxford, from 1976 to 1991, and from 1978 to 1994 was Chancellor of the Open University. His publications include *Victorian People* (1954), *The History of Broadcasting in Britain* (5 vols, 1961–96), *The Age of Improvement, 1783–1867* (1959), *Victorian Cities* (1963), *Victorian Things* (1988) and *A Social History of England* (1983; third edition, 1999). He is President of the Social History Society and of the Victorian Society. He was created a life peer, as Baron Briggs of Lewes, in 1976.

I APPROACHED the formidable task of selecting ten photographs as a historian deeply interested in the century that I have lived through, trying to catch something of its distinctiveness as one century, the last, in a millennium. The order of my sequence of ten matters to me; I am interested both in chronology and in associations attached to images.

Historians are familiar with the problems of selection, but they are seldom tied by regulated restraint. The historical sources for this century are legion, and much that seems to me essential to its understanding has had to be left out, including the two world wars. I would like to have included at least a few photographs that would have referred, if obliquely, to my own experiences, including people working with me at Bletchley, recently publicised as Station X, or in the 1960s at the Open University, which I helped to plan. Its headquarters were located in the new town of Milton Keynes. By the kind of coincidence that we all know in our lives, Bletchley is now part of it.

Born in the north of England, I start there, although as a Yorkshireman in the wrong county, Lancashire. I could not resist a

Mass Observation photograph, however, also for a personal reason. I knew Tom Harrisson, its founder, hosted him at Sussex University when I was Vice-Chancellor, and was responsible for the Mass Observation Archive, invaluable to historians, which is being located at Sussex.

Having spent much of my scholarly life writing about broadcasting, I would like to have included Lord Reith, whom I got to know well, but I settled instead for Lord Northcliffe, who helped to shape mass communications as we now understand them even before this century began, and who died one year after I was born. The role of the media has been crucial to our perception not only of events but of time and space and of entertainment as well as of information.

I felt that I had to include the Channel Tunnel, which fits into a longer story of communications, and the computer, which through the microchip has revolutionised much else besides communications. I had to make use of the first computers at Bletchley before they got their name, but the picture I have chosen to identify my theme is of a computer baby. It was not giant computers but personal ones that signified the biggest change. They were out of sight for most of my life just as mobile phones were out of hearing.

Over the years I have become as much of a cultural as an economic, political or social historian, and I am fascinated by continuity as well as by change. Since the lengthening of the span of life has been a major feature of this century I end with age. The royal family has had to cope more than any other family with relating continuity to change in a process that has always involved the media. What better royal figure to include – and to conclude with – than the Queen Mother, who was born when the century had scarcely begun? Here she is interviewing an old person when she herself was younger. Generations encounter each other, and I believe that they are more revealing time units than decades, centuries or even millennia.

ASA BRIGGS

THERE CAN be no more tempting a placard for a historian except perhaps 'Every Picture Tells A Story'. This photograph was taken for Mass Observation in Bolton Market by Humphrey Spender, around whom whole photographic exhibitions have been organised. The idea of watching people as they 'really were' was Tom Harrisson's, and he was a great bird-watcher before he watched people. Founded in 1937, Mass Observation, recording the present, provided an invaluable archive for the historians of the future. Bolton was a 'Worktown'. The names of most of the observers have been forgotten; so too have the names of the people they observed.

*Truth is Stranger
Than Fiction*
(The Open Market, Bolton)
Humphrey Spender, 1937
Private collection

BORN IN 1865, Alfred Harmsworth created a media dynasty, the House of Northcliffe. His first medium of communication was the bicycle, and the first paper for which he wrote was *Wheel Life*. In 1896 he launched the *Daily Mail*; in 1903 he started the *Daily Mirror*, hailed as 'the women's newspaper'; in 1908 he secretly purchased control of *The Times*; in 1920 he sponsored one of the first radio concerts, with Dame Nellie Melba, 'the Australian nightingale', singing into a microphone at Chelmsford: 'Art and Science joined hands'. Northcliffe, who had most of the faults of a tycoon, loved cars. The one illustrated here is a 28-horsepower 'Lohne Porsche' Mercedes.

Alfred Charles Harmsworth,
1st Viscount Northcliffe
(1865–1922) at his home,
Sutton Place, in Surrey.
Lafayette, 1903
National Portrait Gallery,
London

ASA BRIGGS

Oct. 1906

40

I WANTED to include a woman at the beginning of my sequence, for the role of women has changed fundamentally in this century both in 'the home', a word that survives, and out of it. Where better to start than with a suffragette, campaigning for votes for women and addressing not women but men? The scene, which might have been photographed by an early member of Mass Observation, is Newcastle. (Being a non-Londoner I have deliberately chosen provincial scenes for my ten images whenever possible.) The time is a by-election, October 1908.

By-elections are sometimes more revealing occasions for social historians than general elections. It was the First World War, however, that accelerated the speed of change in the role of women. To the disgust of her more radical daughter, the suffragette leader Emmeline Pankhurst found comfort in the fact that in wartime the suffragette organisation was being used 'to help our country through the period of strain and sorrow'.

ASA BRIGGS

DURING THE First World War large
numbers of men who had never left
Britain before went to fight in the
trenches of France, and during the
Second World War, after the fall of
France, British soldiers made the
dangerous Channel crossing from
Dunkirk. Louis Blériot had already
flown across the Channel in 1909, a
landmark date. It was not until the last
decade of the twentieth century,
however, that the Channel Tunnel, the
Chunnel, an old project, linked Britain
and France for the first time since the
last Ice Age. The treaty authorising the
beginning of work on the tunnel was
signed at Canterbury in February 1986
by Margaret Thatcher, Britain's first
woman prime minister, and President
Mitterrand of France, following a
meeting at Lille in the previous month.

SKIPPING THE Great War and the great Depression – and the Second World War – and sadly leaving out soldiers, sailors, airmen, ATS, WAAFS and the Women's Land Army, not to speak of hunger marchers and Aldermaston marchers, this photograph takes us into what is still the most controversial decade of the twentieth century, the 1960s. Appropriately we move to the sound of rock music, and I have chosen the Stones rather than the Beatles to catch the mood. 'Wait till you see the Stones', a New York socialite exclaimed in 1964, 'They're pure sex! They're divine . . . They're all young and they're taking over, it's like a whole revolution.' Pop culture crossed the Atlantic rather than the Channel – Elvis Presley, Beatles, Stones and all.

The Rolling Stones
for *Beggar's Banquet*
album gatefold.
Clockwise from left:
Charlie Watts (born 1941);
Mick Jagger (born 1943);
Bill Wyman (born 1936);
Brian Jones (1942–69);
Keith Richards
(born 1943)
Michael Joseph, 1968
Iris Kodalith print,
531 x 438mm
National Portrait Gallery,
London

ASA BRIGGS

COAL, IRON and textiles laid the foundations of Britain's industrialisation. George Stephenson, pioneer of the railway, suggested that the Lord Chancellor should not sit on a bag of wool but on a less comfortable bag of coals. With the discovery of new sources of energy – and the decline of Britain's manufacturing industry in the 1970s and 1980s – there was a bitter fight to keep open the pits that had been nationalised after the Second World War. Scargill, the miners' leader, was locked in a bitter struggle in the last of the great coal strikes of the twentieth century in 1984–5, as bitter a struggle as that which followed the abandonment of the miners after the general strike of 1926. This time Margaret Thatcher, not the employees, was the enemy. Symbolically, in 1993 the Queen ceased making the traditional gift of coal to Windsor pensioners.

Arthur Scargill (born 1938)
at the British Steel
Corporation, Orgreave.
Martin Jenkinson,
30 May 1984
Bromide print,
376 × 264mm
National Portrait Gallery,
London

ASA BRIGGS

HOMELESSNESS WAS one of the biggest social issues of the 1980s and 1990s, and it is ironical that it is through this photograph, one of many that I might have chosen, that London makes its way into my selection. It has always been a city of problems, however, as well as a city of prides. Homelessness was associated (just how was debatable) with unemployment.

A Labour politician of the 1960s had claimed that unemployment had at last 'passed into history'. It had not. In 1986 it reached 3.4 million or 14 per cent of the working population. Meanwhile, with homelessness visible, house ownership had doubled since 1951. Every 'sleeping rough' picture doubtless tells its own story. This has been a Big Issue.

Sleeping Rough, London
Jim Barron, 1998
Bromide print,
320 x 413mm
Jim Barron

THE CHARITY on which many people were dependent in the 1980s – to an extent not foreseen in 1945 – was still dependent in considerable measure on religious inspiration. Religion, however, has lost much, though by no means all, of its grip in the twentieth century. This photograph of two of the best known religious figures comes from Liverpool, more of a problem city (Toxteth, political scandal) than London – but also the home of the Beatles. Appropriately it is in a garden that the Anglican bishop of Liverpool, David Sheppard, an ex-England cricketer, and Derek Worlock, the Roman Catholic archbishop, are meeting in ecumenical harmony. The street between their two cathedrals, both new, is called Hope Street. The Anglican cathedral, Gothic, had a Roman Catholic architect; the Roman Catholic, circular, an Anglican one.

Archbishop Derek Worlock (1920–96) and Bishop David Sheppard (born 1929) in Bishop David Sheppard's garden, Liverpool. Stephen Shakeshaft, November 1994 C-type print, 202 × 284mm Stephen Shakeshaft, *Liverpool Daily Post, Liverpool Echo*

ASA BRIGGS

Computer Baby
Michelangelo Gratton,
1990s
Popperfoto

THERE HAVE been twentieth-century generations of computers as well as of human beings, and computers very quickly gave a new connotation to the word 'memory'. The invention of the microchip was as much of a landmark twentieth-century event as the invention of the steam engine in the Industrial Revolution. The revolution associated with the personal computer and most recently with the process of digitalisation – and the Internet – has transformed work and leisure far more than any other twentieth-century development. This not very sophisticated, but none the less attractive picture is evidence of early learning through play. The Internet, democratic but chaotic, came much later. One private citizen proposed as a millennial project that the pattern of a microchip should be displayed/enlarged on a chalk hill as ancient horses were once depicted there by our ancestors. It would symbolise the beginning not only of a new technology but of a new age.

PICTURES OF the Queen Mother abound. This photograph was taken a long time ago in 1961 – appropriately in a garden, like the picture of the two clergymen. The Queen Mother loves gardens, as she loves race courses, and she is shown here visiting a garden in Greenwich, not far from the present site of the Millennium Dome. She is talking to an old lady who for me symbolises increased longevity, a feature of the century (with its hip operations and its transplants), as the Queen Mother herself now does. I would like to have included nurses too. They symbolise not only knowledge and experience but care.

Her Majesty Queen Elizabeth,
The Queen Mother
(born 1900), Greenwich
George Hales,
10 July 1961
Fox Photos/Hulton Getty

ASA BRIGGS

ANNA FORD

BORN IN 1943, Anna Ford studied at Manchester University before teaching at the Rupert Stanley College of Further Education in Belfast and at the Open University. Her broadcasting career began in 1974, when she joined Granada Television as a researcher. She moved to the BBC in 1976, where she worked as a reporter and presenter for *Man Alive* and *Tomorrow's World*. In 1978 she became the first woman newscaster in independent television, for Independent Television News; in the same year she received the TV Times Most Popular TV Personality (Female) award. In 1982 she was a founder-member of TV-AM. She has subsequently worked as a freelance broadcaster and writer, and since 1988 has worked for BBC news and current affairs, presenting the *Six O'Clock News*, the *Today* programme and currently the *One O'Clock News*. She is a Trustee of the Royal Botanic Gardens, Kew, and a former Trustee of the Geffrye Museum.

TO MAKE this daunting task slightly easier, the photographs I've chosen focus entirely on the lives of women. They make up more than half the population but their lives and work have so often been invisible. Unsung, unrecorded and largely unphotographed, the contribution of women to the twentieth century is remarkable. Late in the nineteenth century women were freed from being the property of their husbands, but it was not until the twentieth that they were for the first time legally recognised as citizens. In this century their lives in every respect have been turned upside down. One of the most fundamental changes that has taken place in the last hundred years has been the increasing participation of women in the labour market, particularly the extent to which they have taken up part-time work, where most of them have low-paid jobs, earn less on average than men, while continuing to do the bulk of all household chores. The tradition of man as breadwinner and wife as homemaker has been eroded, and the debate continues between women and men and feminists of every colour as to the different meanings of equality and liberation for each one of us. This century the professions became

ANNA FORD

open to women and gradually each one had their first. The first woman mayor, the first professor, the first MP – though not until 1919 – and the first government minister (Margaret Bondfield) in 1924. But women had to wait until 1942 to head the TUC, 1958 to become a life peer and 1965 to become the first high court judge (Judge Elizabeth Lane). The first woman editor of a major national newspaper (Wendy Henry) was not appointed until 1987, to the *News of the World*. Although we had the first woman prime minister (Margaret Thatcher) in 1979, it was a further eleven years before husbands and wives were independently taxed. And it's only now that black or Asian women are being freed from the prejudices that prevented them from even aspiring to the top. But despite the advances that have been made, women are still under-represented in the ranks of power, policy and decision-making, and many question the whole way in which society and the institutions in it are organised. The search for personal fulfilment, be it happiness, success, wealth or whatever, is pursued by men and women alike, but in these few, idiosyncratically chosen pictures I'd like to celebrate the lives and contribution of women, great and multi-faceted as they are.

May. 21. 1914

EMMELINE PANKHURST was a militant champion of women's suffrage whose forty-year campaign achieved complete success in the year of her death, 1928. Born Emmeline Goulden in Manchester on 14 July 1858, she founded the Women's Social and Political Union in 1903. She was jailed many times and went on hunger strike, being released for a time and then recaptured as soon as she was stronger, under the notorious 'Cat and Mouse Act'. Many who supported suffrage, like Millicent Fawcett, did not believe in violence or militancy, but Emmeline Pankhurst and her followers made immense personal, social and financial sacrifices for their beliefs. Here, on 21 May 1914 (aged 56), she's arrested and carried off from the gates of Buckingham Palace by Superintendent Rolfe. She was driven immediately to Holloway Prison and, as she was being carried past a group of reporters, Mrs Pankhurst called out: 'Arrested at the gates of the Palace. Tell the King!'

Emmeline Pankhurst
(1858–1928) being arrested
by Superintendent Rolfe
outside Buckingham
Palace.

Unknown photographer,
21 May 1914
Museum of London

ANNA FORD

MY MATERNAL grandfather's family came from Salford and Wigan, and many of his male relatives worked in the coal-mines. There was no romance about mining and they wanted a better life for their sons. A fifth of the male work-force left the coalfields in 1914 to join the army and the mines were left dangerously understaffed. The men who stayed worked at the coal-face while surface work was often carried out by women, like these. The war and the work it brought was a new experience for these women, who in their clogs and shawls look humorous, self-confident and strong. My mother's tales of Lancashire women and the tough and self-sacrificing life they led bear this out.

Women coal workers,
Lancashire colliery.
G.P. Lewis,
September 1918
Imperial War Museum

ANNA FORD

WHAT A backbreaking job to carry the family wash to the steamies and then back home to dry and iron it all! I remember my mother washing for seven people, in the days before we had a machine, including all the sheets and every now and then the blankets, in a stone sink in the back kitchen with nothing else but a boiler and a large wooden mangle. Even today with a washing machine it's the sheer boredom of sorting out the same clothes and week after week repetitively washing them. I suppose there must have been a camaraderie in these communal wash-houses, some gossip and laughter to ease the tedium and exhaustion of it all. But what relentlessly tough lives these women led in the pursuit of cleanliness and respectability for their large families. This photograph was taken by Humphrey Spender for a *Picture Post* series on British towns.

'The Steamies' or public wash-house, Glasgow. Humphrey Spender, 1 April 1939 Picture Post/ Hulton Getty

Typing Pool
Keystone Press, *c.*1935
Keystone/Hulton Getty

AS EDUCATIONAL opportunities for women began to expand, growing numbers became equipped with basic office skills. The General Post Office was among the first organisations to employ large numbers of women, largely as clerks. Many women clustered together in predominantly 'female' occupations, in typing pools, as clerks and in banks. They were paid relatively low wages and had limited opportunities for advancement. The typewriter was thought at the time of its introduction to be a further sign of the emancipation of women. This photograph shows women getting on with their work in a typing pool circa 1935. By 1981, 43 per cent of all employed women were clerks. But with routine tasks, low pay and limited aspirations, it does not seem much of an emancipation.

A CLASSIC image of a beautiful woman that shows nothing of the hardships, indignities and heroism of immigrant women who managed to survive in jobs that are still male dominated, and where they stood very little chance of promotion. In the years immediately after the war Britain badly needed plenty of cheap labour for London Transport, the National Health Service, British Rail and the hotel and catering industries. Immigration from the Commonwealth was made easy and the new arrivals came first from the West Indies. For many, difficult conditions were made worse by the prejudiced attitudes of co-workers and bosses alike.

Agatha Claudette Hart,
Bus Conductor,
Stockwell Garage, London.
Dr Heinz Zinram,
14 March 1962
London Transport Museum

ANNA FORD

THIS BOLD and beautiful woman, staring straight into Bailey's lens, is one of the abiding images of the 1960s – along with sleek, well-cut hair, white Courrèges boots, mini-skirts, young women striding along bursting with confidence and a new-found sexual freedom. It was epitomised by such models as Twiggy and Shrimpton, by the designs of Mary Quant, the hair-styles of Vidal Sassoon, the music of the Stones, the Beatles, Marianne Faithfull and Janis Joplin, and the student demonstrations of 1968. It was the decade in which I left home, was a sort of radical student, played my guitar wherever I went and ran out of a Sassoon hair salon when they insisted I have their geometric cut. The King's Road and Carnaby Street were meccas, as was the L.S.E., where the most radical ideas were being hammered out. But was this also the decade that focused our attention on our looks, the preoccupation that Germaine Greer argues goes some way towards ruining our lives?

Jean Shrimpton
(born 1943)
David Bailey,
November 1963
David Bailey

ANNA FORD

THE PUBLISHING firm of Virago, founded in 1973 by Carmen Callil, achieved more for women's literature than any other. Specialising in books by or about women, in addition to new works, it re-discovered largely forgotten books by leading women authors, and re-issued them. The name of the firm was a clever play on words, a virago originally being a heroic Amazon woman, rather than the more abusive, and in recent times more common, reference to a shrewish woman.

Founding Directors of the Virago Press. Left to right: Harriet Spicer; Ursula Owen; Lennie Goodings; Alexandra Pringle; Carmen Callil. Susan Greenhill, 5 July 1988 Susan Greenhill

ANNA FORD

FRINK'S GREAT bronze birds, larger than life-size striding figures and men on horseback are some of the outstanding sculptural works of our age. She was a very powerful artist, and a gentle and sympathetic woman. Her *Tribute Heads* (1975–7) were all meant to represent people suffering for their beliefs, and grew from her horror at acts of inhumanity. Most of her figures were male yet bore a strange physical resemblance to her, with their strong waistless bodies. I would have liked here to show a group photograph, if it existed, of some of our outstanding women artists. It would have included Sheila Fell, Paula Rego, Prunella Clough, Mary Fedden, Mary Newcombe, Bridget Riley, Gillian Ayres, Rachel Whiteread and many others.

Dame Elisabeth Frink
(1930–93) in her studio,
Dorset.
David Buckland,
May 1990
Cibachrome print,
950 x 760mm
National Portrait Gallery,
London (x47160)

FOR SOME reason women are not really supposed to be funny; it's traditionally a man's world, but this team invented a completely new kind of humour for the television series *Absolutely Fabulous*. It's remembered line by line by many teenagers, based on the wonderfully neurotic Edina (Jennifer Saunders), doyen of the fashion world, and her chain-smoking, champagne-swilling, blaspheming friend Patsy (Joanna Lumley). Saffron, Eddie's daughter (Julia Sawalha), is the only grown-up, and Eddie's mother (June Whitfield) is much more knowing than she lets on. Bubbles (Jane Horrocks) is one of the great quirky inventions of modern comedy. They are indeed absolutely fabulous, and written by the hugely talented Jennifer Saunders.

Jennifer Saunders (born 1958) and Joanna Lumley (born 1946) as Edina and Patsy in *Absolutely Fabulous*.
Trevor Leighton, 1996
Cibachrome print,
293 x 293mm
National Portrait Gallery,
London

ANNA FORD

69

Mo Mowlam (born 1949)
John Giles, 2 June 1998
John Giles/'PA' Photos

I LIKE Mo Mowlam because she is often blissfully unaware of herself. The lack of vanity in her ability to appear as Secretary of State for Northern Ireland without a wig when her own hair has not yet regrown after her treatment for a brain tumour is just wonderful. One of the least stuffy of politicians, she's also a woman who at 48 landed the gravest job, that of trying to keep alive the hopes for peace amongst a community still riven with suspicion and mistrust. The fact that a workable peace can come only from the people themselves makes her job even more difficult, but her courage impresses all sections of the community. I lived and taught in Belfast between 1970 and 1974. Some of my students were internees and I regularly visited Long Kesh to take classes. It was not until then that I even began to understand the profoundly different standpoints taken by people with diametrically differing views on religion, their own history, culture and use of language, and who had no meeting places in which to discuss those differences. Things have come a long way in the last thirty years and Mo Mowlam will be remembered for her feisty part in their progress.

ANNA FORD

MAX HASTINGS

MY IMAGES of the century are not designed simply as a gallery of the famous or powerful. I have excluded politicians, because so few exercise lasting influence upon their times. I searched for people instead who have made a difference, or whose images reflect a mood, a spirit, a popular trend. Heroes have their place, but so also do rogues and sinners. Haig is there, because the unspeakable experience of the First World War must be reflected. So too must the Royal Navy, and show business, and that enduring extension of show business, the Church of England's resident flock of black sheep. We should not despise the clubland heroes of John Buchan, whom schoolboys could admire without embarrassment in the age of the Empire. The century's literary genius is best represented by Evelyn Waugh, and eccentric genius is reflected by Vita Sackville-West. There must also be people whose very names remain unknown to us, the representatives of the millions who have no place in the *Dictionary of National Biography*, or even upon the captions of photographs, but who were typical of the century in a way that the famous were not. They were as important as the great warriors and artists. In the next century, we are likely to be celebrating new kinds of people – environmentalists rather than soldiers, sportsmen rather than explorers, singers rather than proconsuls. Any future list is likely to be less nationalistic, more focused upon perception rather than territorial conquest. Arguably, the twentieth has been the last century in which men and women who felt no shame in enfolding themselves in the Union Jack could take pride of place among figures of influence. This is no cause for regret, but only for reflection. It is droll to consider that at least half of those who feature among my own images of the past hundred years would have felt insulted, during their own lifetimes, had they not felt sure of their own claims upon posterity. The others would be astonished to know that they are remembered and celebrated at all.

THE REVEREND Harold Davidson is the outstanding example of the naughty vicar, who has enriched so many British newspaper proprietors through the century. Rector of Stiffkey in Norfolk, for years Davidson maintained an astoundingly energetic double life, taking services on Sunday and spending the rest of the week pursuing pretty girls through the streets and bedrooms of London. His trial by a Church Court lasted for most of 1932, and details of his career as 'the prostitutes' padre' – his own boast – delighted the nation. His subsequent unfrocking might have proved an anti-climax, but he went on to address sympathisers from a barrel on Blackpool pier, and ended his career in 1937 as the last Christian known to have been devoured by lions, after he rashly sought to harangue an audience from a circus cage. His remains were belatedly retrieved by a teenage female lion-tamer.

The Reverend Harold
Davidson (1875–1937),
Rector of Stiffkey, Norfolk
Associated Press,
20 May 1932
Topham/Associated Press

MAX HASTINGS

A PART of the genius of *Picture Post*, the magazine that created photo-journalism in Britain, is that it captured public behaviour for posterity as never before. Before 1939, photography focused chiefly upon the great and the famous. *Picture Post* tells us how ordinary people were living, loving, working, playing and dying. The girls on the Caterpillar present a perfect portrait of exuberance without inhibition in the innocent age of Butlin's holiday camps and all the fun of the fair, when the working class was still thrilled to discover that it was allowed to enjoy itself at all.

The Caterpillar,
Southend Fair.
Kurt Hutton,
8 October 1938
Picture Post/
Hulton Getty

MAX HASTINGS

EVELYN WAUGH, born in 1903, was the
most important English novelist of
the twentieth century. He burst on the
scene very young – one of his best
books, *Decline and Fall* (1928), was
published when he was 24, followed by
Vile Bodies (1930). This picture catches
perfectly the young Oxford prodigy
of the Roaring Twenties, the sharp,
lacerating intelligence of his features
already betraying a hint of the
misanthropy that became so
pronounced in Waugh a few years
later. Embittered by the failure of his
first marriage and with a growing
distaste for modern life, he proved a
disastrous wartime officer who none
the less wrote the outstanding British
novel sequence about the experience
of the Second World War, 'Sword of
Honour'. He died in 1966.

Evelyn Waugh (1903–66),
Magdalene Bridge,
Oxford.
Unknown photographer,
1925
Auberon Waugh

MAX HASTINGS

NO SINGLE photograph better captures
the spirit of the post-war Welfare State
and Labour-governed Britain than the
image of the little boy in his National
Health Service spectacles. Hope,
courage, mischief and impish charm
are printed deep upon the face of this
offspring of generations of poverty and
deprivation. Forget for a moment that
the Welfare State was an act of
economic folly launched with
borrowed money, using American cash
that more prudent European nations
used for industrial investment. The
case for what Clement Attlee's
government did to transform
the fortunes of the British people is
better expressed by this image than by
a thousand words.

National Health Specs,
Princess Theatre,
Glasgow.
Haywood Magee,
1 November 1951
Picture Post/
Hulton Getty

MAX HASTINGS

JOHN BUCHAN was a Scots son of the manse who became the most popular thriller-writer of his generation, and also scaled the summits of the British establishment. The author of *The Thirty-Nine Steps* (1915), he idolised the rulers of the British Empire – after a notable Oxford career, he served as one of 'Lord Milner's young men' in South Africa – and revelled in 'the great game' played by clean-limbed young Englishmen on the frontiers of civilisation. Few men have written better about rural Britain – and Africa – or about the shooting and fishing that he loved. His novels retain their period charm, though his lack of humour and relentless social alpinism irked even some of his contemporaries. When he was appointed Governor-General of Canada in 1935, the government suggested that he would be best received by the Canadians as a commoner. Buchan invoked a dying parent to plead for a title, cabling the Prime Minister: 'An immediate peerage might revive mother.' He died as 1st Baron Tweedsmuir in 1940.

John Buchan, 1st Baron
Tweedsmuir (1875–1940)
fishing on the
Cascapedia River, Quebec.
Unknown photographer,
1936
Lord Tweedsmuir

MAX HASTINGS

85

HEROISM IN arms is out of fashion, but no single figure more perfectly represents the *beau ideal* of the mid-century English hero than Kenneth More as the legless air ace Douglas Bader in the film *Reach for the Sky*. More's charm romanticised Bader, whose ruthless personality in real life frightened as many people as it impressed. Bader lost his legs in a rash feat of low-level acrobatics with the pre-war RAF, but forced his way back into the air in the crisis of 1940, and went on to lead a fighter wing before he was shot down and captured by the Germans. Even then, he attempted to escape and ended the war in Colditz Castle. More was the film star adored by a generation as the brave, honest, open and handsome exemplar of what the British people of the 1940s and 1950s wanted themselves to be. *Reach for the Sky* represents his finest achievement.

Kenneth More (1914–82) as Douglas Bader in *Reach for the Sky.* Charles Trigg, 1956 Bromide print, 511 x 418mm National Portrait Gallery, London (x34536)

MAX HASTINGS

IT IS unthinkable to represent twentieth-century Britain without a representative of the Royal Navy, the greatest seagoing force in the world before the 1940s. The three most famous British naval officers of the past 200 years – Nelson, Beatty and Mountbatten – were all notable bounders ashore. Beatty was seldom photographed without his naval cap at the cad's rakish angle. While his celebrity during and after the First World War matched that of Nelson, his abilities as an admiral did not. He was a bold and dashing leader of the battle-cruiser squadron, and later of the entire Grand Fleet. But his achievements in battle never matched his fame. A spoilt darling of fortune, he married the daughter of the Chicago millionaire Marshall Field. When he was threatened with disgrace for wrecking the engines of his destroyer in the Mediterranean before the war, his outraged wife declared: 'Court-martial my David? I'll buy them another damn ship.'

MAX HASTINGS

AS COMMANDER-IN-CHIEF of the British Expeditionary Force in France from 1915 to 1918, Field Marshal Earl Haig (as he became) was the symbol of Britain's military commitment to the First World War and – to post-war generations – of the ghastly slaughter that this embraced. An archetypal cavalry officer of the period, he was an intriguer who exploited his friendship with King George V as vigorously as his hatred of politicians. He is seen here with Lloyd George and the French socialist politician Albert Thomas, 'frocks' whom he disliked and distrusted more than most. Haig was the last British battlefield commander to be rewarded from public funds as well as with public honours when victory came. Historians who defend him argue, justly, that he was an admirable administrator of his huge forces, and that none of his contemporaries would have been better able to break the stalemate of the trenches. But Haig's insensitivity to the fate of hundreds of thousands of the men under his command today attracts less admiration than his Roman stoicism aroused among his contemporaries.

Sir Douglas Haig (1861–1928), David Lloyd George (1863–1945), General Joffre (1852–1931) and Albert Thomas (1878–1932), Mesulte, France.
Unknown photographer, 12 September 1916
Hulton Getty

MAX HASTINGS

VITA SACKVILLE-WEST was a forgettable
novelist, but a hugely memorable
personality. A daughter of the great
Sackville family of Knole, she married
the diplomat and diarist Harold
Nicolson in 1913. Their remarkable
alliance, itself a monument to high
culture, survived the homosexuality
of both – Vita conducted a notable
relationship with the novelist Virginia
Woolf. But her greatest claim on
posterity stems from her achievement
as a gardener. With her husband, she
created one of England's greatest
gardens at Sissinghurst Castle in Kent,
and her writing about gardening is
among the finest of the century. She
stands foremost among the handful
of deeply influential figures who have
made the English a nation of tillers
and weeders.

Vita Sackville-West
(1892–1962)
Cecil Beaton, 1958
Bromide print,
240 x 207mm
National Portrait Gallery,
London (x14197)

MAX HASTINGS

Lew Grade, Baron Grade
(1906–98)
Snowdon,
15 November 1997

LEW GRADE epitomised the great tradition of the Jewish show-business promoter, who also became one of the best-loved figures in the British entertainment industry. The eldest of three successful sons of Russian immigrants, Isaac and Olga Winogradsky, Grade first ventured on to the boards as a professional dancer. His career lifted into the big time when he sunk everything he owned into commercial television at its foundation in the 1950s, and became one of its major forces. He was master of the one-liner – he remarked of his disastrous film *Raise The Titanic* (1980): 'It would have been cheaper to lower the Atlantic' – and a highly successful salesman of popular British television series abroad. Never seen without a giant cigar, the man who loved a deal was still capable of showing a deft shoe to the photographer into his nineties. Lord Grade died in 1998 at the age of 91.

STEPHEN HAWKING

BORN IN 1942, Stephen Hawking was educated at St Alban's School before reading physics at University College, Oxford, graduating in 1962. He then moved to Cambridge to work on a PhD on relativity theory in the Department of Applied Mathematics and Theoretical Physics. He was elected a Fellow of Gonville and Caius College in 1965, and became Lucasian Professor of Mathematics at the University of Cambridge in 1979. He is best known for his work on the theory of black holes. His publications include *The Large Scale Structure of Space-Time* (with G.F.R. Ellis, 1973), the best-selling *A Brief History of Time* (1988) and *Black Holes and Baby Universes* (1993). Since the 1960s he has suffered from the increasingly debilitating motor neurone disease. He was elected a Fellow of the Royal Society in 1974, and became a Companion of Honour in 1989.

MY SELECTION of pictures concentrates on scientists and women, whom I consider the important members of society. The work of British scientists has helped to change the world, yet how many people know of the physicists Rutherford or Dirac, the biophysicist Crick or the microbiologist Fleming? Being the only scientist among the selectors, I first thought that I should have a list entirely of British scientists. However, I found that I was getting down to the 'B team' at the bottom of my list. I therefore decided to celebrate excellence in another area. Even though I strongly disagreed with many of her policies, Margaret Thatcher was a must, as was Princess Diana. My aim was to show some of the outstanding British faces of this century.

STEPHEN HAWKING

Francis Crick (on right;
born 1916), with
James Watson (born 1928)
Antony Barrington
Brown, 21 May 1953
Modern bromide print
from original negative,
247 × 299mm
National Portrait Gallery,
London (x45733)

INSPIRED GUESSWORK led Francis Crick and James Watson to the double helix structure of DNA, in 1953. This discovery would change the world, because it established the molecular basis of inheritance and made genetic engineering possible.

EMMELINE PANKHURST helped to make
Britain a democracy, a result that was
not achieved until 1928, when all
women over the age of 21 finally got
the right to vote.

Emmeline Pankhurst
(1858–1928)
Olive Edis, 1920s
Sepia platinotype print,
202 x 150mm
National Portrait Gallery,
London (x6195)

DIRAC, WORKING at Cambridge during the 1920s, was one of the main architects of quantum theory, which has transformed our view of reality itself and is fundamental to the electronics industry. If he had patented the Dirac equation, which governs the electron, he would have become a billionaire, with a royalty on every television, computer and mobile phone.

Paul Dirac (1902–84)
Edward Leigh, 1950s
Department of Applied
Mathematics and
Theoretical Physics, The
University of Cambridge

STEPHEN HAWKING

I DISAGREED with many of her policies
but I can't help admiring her. Who else
would have got back the Falklands and
made both sides of industry face up to
the real world?

The Rt. Hon. Margaret
Thatcher (born 1925)
Norman Parkinson, 1981
Cibachrome print,
298 x 244mm
National Portrait Gallery,
London (x30176)

STEPHEN HAWKING

A BRILLIANT mathematician and philosopher, Bertrand Russell realised the danger that the world was in from nuclear weapons during the Cold War. With supposedly responsible politicians talking calmly of megadeaths, his was one of the few voices of sanity.

Bertrand Russell,
3rd Earl Russell
(1872–1970)
Ida Kar, 1953
Vintage bromide print,
241 x 194mm
National Portrait Gallery,
London (x13796)

STEPHEN HAWKING

THE MOST intelligent novelist of her generation. No wonder that at the end of Edward Albee's play *Who's Afraid of Virginia Woolf* (1964) one of the two main characters says: 'I am'.

Virginia Woolf
(1882–1941)
George Charles
Beresford, 1902
Platinum print,
152 x 108mm
National Portrait Gallery,
London (P221)

STEPHEN HAWKING

IN 1906 Rutherford discovered that matter is not continuous but made up of atoms, in which electrons orbit a compact nucleus. This is the basis of all modern physics, chemistry and electronics.

Ernest Rutherford (on right; 1871–1937) and Hans Wilhelm Geiger (1882–1945)
Unknown photographer, 1910s
UK Atomic Energy Authority

Sir Alexander Fleming
(1881–1955), St Mary's
Hospital, London.
Dr Peter N. Cardew, 1950s
Alexander Fleming
Laboratory Museum and
St Mary's Hospital
Medical School
Audiovisual Services

SIR ALEXANDER Fleming discovered
penicillin, the first antibiotic. It was
developed with great speed for military
reasons during the Second World War.
It must have saved more lives than
were lost in the war.

ALAN TURING was the first person to formulate the theory of computers, in 1936. The argument continues as to whether there is an essential difference between a Turing machine and a human brain, and whether a computer can show true intelligence. I believe it can.

Alan Turing (1912–54)
Elliott & Fry, March 1951
162 x 117mm
National Portrait Gallery,
London (x27079)

STEPHEN HAWKING

NO QUESTION that this is one of the
faces of the century.

Diana, Princess of Wales
(1961–97)
Snowdon, 1981
Cibachrome,
508 x 406mm
National Portrait Gallery,
London (P218)

STEPHEN HAWKING

HELENA KENNEDY

BORN IN Glasgow in 1950, Helena Kennedy studied law in London and was called to the Bar at Gray's Inn in 1972; she became a QC in 1991, and was a member of the Bar Council from 1990 to 1993. She has served on various councils, commissions and committees. In 1994 she became Chancellor of Oxford Brookes University and in 1996 President of Hillcroft College. She has presented many radio and television programmes, including *Heart of the Matter* (BBC, 1987), and in 1988 created the television drama series *Blind Justice*. She was a joint author of *The Bar on Trial* (1978), *Child Abuse within the Family* (1984) and *Balancing Acts* (1989), and in 1992 published *Eve was Framed*. She was created a life peer, as Baroness Kennedy of the Shaws, in 1997. She is now Chair of the British Council and President of the National Children's Bureau.

WHEN ASKED to choose images of the twentieth century that reflected Britain, I instinctively found myself choosing themes rather than individuals. In a century scarred with the horror of world wars, genocide and monstrous testaments to man's inhumanity, other themes shine through with evidence of our better selves: the creation of the Welfare State, the anti-war movement, the concept of social justice, the considerable steps towards women's equality and the efforts to end racial discrimination.

The main struggles of the twentieth century have been concerned with rights. Just as democratic rights dominated the beginning of the century, so human rights have become the focus at the end. As the century closes we are still trying to find a resolution in Ireland, still being shocked at the horrors of war, still seeking solutions to the division between rich and poor, still trying to tackle physical and sexual abuse and pursuing the means to protect minorities.

HELENA KENNEDY

Yet the gains have been enormous. It was not only our grand-mothers who lacked the vote at the beginning of the century. My grandfathers too, as working-class men, were disenfranchised. My grandparents and those of most British citizens had only a very elementary education, but now their great-grandchildren have a decent chance of going to university. The lives of previous generations were taken up with intense physical labour, industrial and domestic; now most forms of work have been radically transformed.

If the century has shown us anything, it is that human beings have extraordinary resilience, but it has also shown us the moral imperative of improving everyone's life chances and removing divisions between people.

Mary Phillips (third from left, second row; 1880–1969) on her release from Holloway Prison, London.
Unknown photographer, 23 August 1908
Museum of London

I CAME across this photograph when I was making a television programme called *Time, Gentleman, Please!* in Scotland. Scottish women were very active in the suffragette movement and at the forefront of efforts to gain admission for women to the universities and the professions. However, they also led the egalitarian argument that the franchise should not just be extended to women of the propertied classes but should include all adult men and women. They made common cause with political activists such as Keir Hardie, the founder of the Labour Party, in the campaign for universal suffrage. This is a photograph taken outside Holloway Prison in London on the release of Mary Phillips in 1908; she had been sentenced to imprisonment for obstructing the police at a demonstration in Parliament Square. The doughty figure in the middle is 'General' Drummond, the Germaine Greer of her day.

HELENA KENNEDY

British tear-gas victims,
Béthune, France.
Unknown photographer,
April 1918
Imperial War Museum

MY OWN grandfather, a young Irish soldier with the Dublin Fusiliers, was killed just five days after the start of the First World War. My grandmother received the news that he had been blown to pieces as she was going into labour with her first baby, my father. There are no 'virtual' wars, even in the late twentieth century. In an age when civilian deaths in war are spoken of as collateral damage it is important to remind ourselves of the real cost of wars, even when the rationale for engagement is just.

HELENA KENNEDY

THE ISSUE of Ireland has haunted this century. The faltering efforts to seek a resolution in 1922 led to civil war and allegations of betrayal, and no doubt the lessons of the past hang heavy upon the present efforts to secure a lasting peace. This is a photograph of Michael Collins, the Sinn Fein leader, addressing a huge rally in Dublin at College Green after signing the Treaty establishing the Irish Free State. He was killed within a few months.

The image also reminds us forcefully how the direct, face to face, nature of political communication has largely become a thing of the past, given the uses of modern technology.

HELENA KENNEDY

125

HELENA KENNEDY

WHEN THE Second World War ended in 1945, British troops entered Belsen, one of the Nazi concentration camps. What met their eyes defied description. The archive of photographs taken by the soldiers who removed charred remains from mass graves, cleaned out gas chambers and helped the remaining few into the blinking light of freedom bears a permanent witness to the horror. The images that were considered fit for publication became seared on the minds of my parents' generation. The outrages of the Holocaust shocked the world and, in the spirit that 'never again' should such crimes against humanity occur or go unpunished, the *Universal Declaration of Human Rights* was drafted and signed in 1948. It is the most radical document of the twentieth century, establishing human rights as values, capable of existing independently of religions or ideologies.

THE PHOTOGRAPHER Bert Hardy was one
of the great photo-journalists of the
century, preferring to document the
lives of ordinary people, especially the
poor. Despite all the material gains of
the twentieth century, almost three out
of ten children live below the poverty
line in Britain today. They have been
retitled the 'socially excluded' but
basically they are poor. This
photograph taken in Glasgow's Gorbals
in the late 1940s could be reproduced
in most of our inner cities today.

The Gorbals, Glasgow.
Bert Hardy,
31 January 1948
The Photographers'
Gallery, London

HELENA KENNEDY

THE CREATION of the Welfare State in the aftermath of the Second World War was the sign of a maturing democracy recognising that social justice is an essential component of any civilised nation. My mother still speaks with reverential tones about the creation of the National Health Service and the determination of Nye Bevan to bring it into being. One of her brothers had died of scarlet fever as a baby and there was lifelong breast-beating by my grandmother at not having kept aside enough money to afford the doctor at the first sign of illness. Every expenditure was carefully measured and she blamed herself that she had bought shoes for another child with their only savings. The National Health Service, a bold universal benefit, was at the heart of the Welfare State and it has now become such a national treasure that any political leader threatens it at his or her peril!

Aneurin Bevan
(1897–1960) at Park
Hospital, Davyhulme,
Lancashire.
Unknown photographer,
1947
Mirror Syndication
International

THE CAPTION below this photograph when it was published in 1953 read:

Mrs X has just had her twentieth baby. He is already an uncle to her older daughter's children, and the entire family lives together in a terraced house in Holloway, north London. Mr X earns £9 per week, plus a little overtime, as a kitchen cabinet sprayer and they receive £2 16s. family allowance. But with the family devouring fifty-two pounds of potatoes a week, fourteen loaves of bread, and each of the younger children getting pocket money every Saturday, that doesn't stretch very far.

There are undoubtedly great joys to be found in large families but one of the most liberating changes for women this century has been the ability to control their fertility. The availability of family planning and contraception has radically altered lives and relationships in a positive way. The fear of pregnancy and the inability to care adequately for too many children was an enormous burden on families and no amount of romanticising should ever deny the reality.

Charles and Elizabeth Hudson, with some of their twenty children and six grandchildren, London.
Kurt Hutton,
24 September 1953
Picture Post/
Hulton Getty

HELENA KENNEDY

VANESSA REDGRAVE and Tariq Ali in 1968 demonstrating in Grosvenor Square against the war in Vietnam. It is now fashionable to decry the 1960s and 1970s as a period that belonged to the 'me' generation, with self-indulgence as the by-word. In fact, they were decades marked by concern about the corrosive effect of class division and inequality and Third World poverty. It was a time when having a social conscience did not mean being dismissed as a wet or a bleeding heart, when the civil rights movement and the second wave of feminism began, and when young people took to the streets to register their horror at an unjust war. If there was an eruption of free love it was not happening where I lived in Glasgow!

Tariq Ali (born 1937) and Vanessa Redgrave (born 1937), Anti-Vietnam War demonstration, Grosvenor Square, London.
John Walmsley, 17 March 1968
Bromide fibre print, 203 x 137mm
National Portrait Gallery, London (x6394)

HELENA KENNEDY

ONE OF the great triumphs at the end of the century is that more and more women are able to fulfil their aspirations and participate in all walks of life. Wonderful, effective women are making a difference to our world and inspiring other women. I love this photograph of Glenys Kinnock and Joan Ruddock MP, demonstrating at the Molesworth cruise missile site, looking strong, beautiful and happy.

Glenys Kinnock (born 1944) and Joan Ruddock (born 1943), CND demonstration, Molesworth cruise missile site, Cambridgeshire.
Neil Libbert, February 1985
Neil Libbert

HELENA KENNEDY

OUR BEST hope for the future is education. It changed my life and I still get a lump in my throat when I attend diploma or graduation ceremonies. The growth in higher education in the last decade has been incredible, with huge increases in the number of women and mature students. However, still too few people from disadvantaged backgrounds are going on to college or university.

Education has always been a source of social vitality and the more people we can include in the community of learning, whether in further or higher education, the greater the benefits to us all. The very process involves interaction between people; it is the means by which the values and wisdom of a society are shared and transmitted across generations. Education strengthens the ties that bind people, takes the fear out of difference and encourages tolerance. It helps people see what makes the world tick and the ways in which they, individually and together, can make a difference. It is also the likeliest means of creating a modern, well-skilled work-force, reducing crime and creating participating citizens. What more convincing do we need? The by-words for the twenty-first century must be 'Learning Works!'

Graduate, North East
Surrey College of
Technology, Fairfield
Halls, Croydon.
Colin Edwards,
February 1999
Colin Edwards/
Photofusion

HELENA KENNEDY

TREVOR PHILLIPS

BORN IN 1953, the broadcaster and journalist Trevor Phillips attended schools in London and Georgetown, Guyana, and Imperial College, London. He was President of the National Union of Students from 1978 to 1980. He began his television career in 1980, as a researcher for London Weekend Television. He subsequently produced, amongst other series, *Black on Black*, then in 1986 became a reporter for *This Week*. He was editor of the *London Programme* for London Weekend Television from 1987 to 1992, and then Head of Current Affairs. He is currently a presenter for the *London Programme*, *Crosstalk* and *The Material World*, and Chairman of the London Arts Board. He was a recipient of RTS Awards in 1988, 1993 and 1998. In 1998 with his brother Mike he published *Windrush: The Irresistable Rise of Multi-Racial Britain*.

IN THE late 1980s I stood in a packed church in the American South, and repeated the three words uttered again and again by the preacher, Jesse Jackson: 'I am somebody'. It was at that moment that I finally understood what democracy meant. In one blinding, liberating moment I realised that it wasn't just about the right to vote. It was about the fact that no-one could tell me what I should be or do, and that I need not be trapped by the place of my birth, or the colour of my skin, or what others thought I should be like. This series of photographs represents for me the story of the way in which people have fought to be seen as individuals, and to be treated as equals, whatever their backgrounds. But it also explores the risks and responsibilities that come with freedom.

When I was born, on a New Year's Eve just after the middle of the century, the future of most London babies born that night could be plotted with some confidence from a knowledge of our parents' addresses and occupations, our race and our sex. Most of us would live where our parents did, follow the same trades as our fathers or mothers, and we would know our places.

TREVOR PHILLIPS

When I was aged nine or ten, my father took me to see his 'office', a vast sorting-room in the General Post Office's main London building. We stood on the edge of the floor watching scores of uniformed, mainly black, men despatching the nation's mail. As a smartly dressed civilian marched through the ranks of the sorters, my father said matter-of-factly: 'There's one of the guv'nors'. I recall no envy or anger in his voice; merely the acceptance that he, a black man, who had left school at fourteen and taught himself all he knew, would never be a 'guv'nor'.

As we reach the close of the century, such deference seems more than a lifetime away. It is inconceivable that my two daughters or anyone of their generation would allow their lives to be determined by others' expectations. Yet their great-great grandmothers did. What happened in between?

The twentieth century did not have to be a period that gave more people more choice and more control both over their own lives and what the state did to them. Fascism did not have to be defeated. The

Berlin Wall did not have to come down. But these things happened, and they pointed towards the possibility of a world in which human solidarity and the desire to be free are not mere abstractions. This series of images cannot possibly capture it all; but it reflects my belief that over these remarkable hundred years we have thrown off the stifling cloak of deference, prejudice and social inertia because of the genius, sacrifice and courage of millions of individuals.

TREVOR PHILLIPS

THE LAST unchallenged monarch of
the Empire – on which the sun would
never set – and what we would now
call his chief spin doctor in
conference. If the King was the symbol
of the dominance over millions of
people across the globe, it was at least
in part because the powerful works
of imagination wrought by Kipling
persuaded even the subjected that they
were better off under the guidance of a
superior people. It was the sunset of
the period during which monarchs and
governments could do as they liked –
and we would simply accept that they
knew better. The photograph also
demonstrates the distance between
the King and everyone else; only his
favourite stands close to him.

Rudyard Kipling
(1865–1936) and King
George V (1865–1936)
Daily Sketch
photographer, 1910s
Bromide print,
220 x 149mm
National Portrait Gallery,
London (x36220)

THIS IMAGE captures the beginning of the end of Empire. The Mountbattens were liked in India, probably because they never minded having to rub shoulders with the Indians. They are sitting in the Governor-General's garden at a farewell event. They have no platform, nothing separates them from the crowd; indeed, it is almost as though they are already disappearing under the democratic tide. The British went to great lengths to emphasise their difference from and superiority over the natives – one has only to watch the film *Sanders of the River* (1935) to see how Africa was made into the 'white man's burden'. But here, the only mark of the Governor-General's status is the ornate sofa (why is it in the garden? Talk about 'mad dogs and Englishmen'!), which is shared by the man who had already effectively taken over Mountbatten's powers – Jawaharlal Nehru, India's first prime minister.

Earl Mountbatten of Burma (1900-79), Viceroy of India, and his wife Countess Mountbatten of Burma (1901-60), Vicereine of India, hosting a farewell party for Government House staff, Delhi.
Unknown photographer, 19 June 1948
Trustees of the Broadlands Archives

TREVOR PHILLIPS

MOST OF those who came from the Caribbean after the Second World War were simply adventurous young people who had volunteered to fight against Hitler and were returning for one last fling in England before settling down. The *Empire Windrush* brought 492 of them, and 8 stowaways, in June 1948, docking at Tilbury. Half had been in the RAF, mostly mechanics who had kept the planes flying during the Battle of Britain, though there were some pilots. Most thought that they would be home again in a few years. They stayed and became the advance guard of what has now become a more or less completely British community. Without them it is unlikely that I would be here to make this selection at all.

Passengers on the
Empire Windrush
Unknown photographer,
22 June 1948
Topham Picture Point

PRIOR TO Shirley Bassey's explosion into show business, most non-white performers were American or Caribbean – the dancer Josephine Baker, the bandleader 'Snakehips' Johnson or Paul Robeson. When Bassey moved from being a Tiger Bay starlet to a 1960s sex bomb, she broke out of the stuffy mould of British entertainment, giving the business colour, charisma, brashness and a hint of wildness. She was one of the first tabloid stars, and has managed to win respect without being totally respectable. She and Robeson also share a link to Wales, a country in which I've always felt at home, since virtually everyone there is called either Trevor, or Phillips . . .

Shirley Bassey
(born 1937)
Koo Stark, 1992
Toned bromide fibre
print, 356 x 353mm
National Portrait Gallery,
London

TREVOR PHILLIPS

149

FREUD'S EXPLORATIONS into the human psyche probably did more than any other piece of scientific work to release people in the West from the straitjacket of Victorian ignorance and fear. We often forget that he was a physician; his pioneering studies were conducted in order to release patients from conditions they did not understand.

Symptoms that a century ago would have been held in check by powerful social codes and, where necessary, physical repression were the subject of analysis. This photograph is especially powerful and unusual. Freud peers at us directly and somewhat uncertainly; it is as though he himself is in our dreams.

Sigmund Freud (1856–1939) at his London home, 39 Elsworthy Road, Hampstead. Unknown photographer, 1938 Freud Museum, London

TREVOR PHILLIPS

Sir Oswald Mosley
(third from left;
1896–1980), William
Joyce, 'Lord Haw-Haw'
(far left; 1906–46) and
other members of the
British Union of Fascists.
Unknown photographer,
c.1935
Keystone/Hulton Getty

INDIVIDUAL FREEDOM and liberty of expression are not an unmixed blessing. Democracies also include the bigoted, the prejudiced and the vicious. The century has liberated some of the best in human kind; it has also released some of the worst in us. There has to be a place for downright evil in this series, alongside the myriad positive achievements. Among the British fascists, Mosley could at least claim that he had a political theory, and that he did not know what had been taking place in the concentration camps. William Joyce, 'Lord Haw-Haw', could offer no such excuse. His propaganda broadcasts for the Nazis were born of a mixture of self-aggrandisement and sheer wickedness – an old-fashioned word for a quality that survives. Joyce used a great medium to mask one of the great crimes of modern times.

TREVOR PHILLIPS

PERSONAL FREEDOM is not only about the right to do as we choose. It also requires us to choose to do what is right. As the shackles of social constraints have been shed, some people have abused that freedom in almost unimaginable ways. Ian Brady came to stand for evil in our society. It is not only that he wantonly tortured and murdered children. It is that for millions of people he poisoned the trust that ought to exist between adults and children; the 'Moors' murders marked the moment at which children began to be thought of as being in danger when not in their parents' sight. As a result, children no longer have the freedoms that many enjoyed in the earlier years of this century. Paradoxically, greater freedom for adults has led to virtual house arrest for today's children. Oddly, in the photograph Brady himself looks a picture of innocence, and seems hardly more than a boy.

Ian Brady (born 1938) after his arrest for the 'Moors' murders. William H. Alden, 22 October 1965 *Evening Standard/* Hulton Getty

TREVOR PHILLIPS

I CHOSE the picture of the fans rather than the Fab Four because, no matter how talented and musical they were, the Beatles will be remembered as much for the social change they marked as for their tunes. This picture is a remarkable spectacle. A crowd of young girls is confronted with two of the most potent symbols of the British Establishment: the police and the gates of Buckingham Palace. Lennon, McCartney, Harrison and Starr are inside receiving their MBEs, itself the mark of admission to the top people's club. Do they stand demurely and respectfully, with eyes cast down waiting for the boys to emerge? Do they hell! The Beatles belong to the people, who are determined to claim them back from the stuffy Palace. The struggle, though real, is evidently good-natured. The policemen accept that the days when they could claim automatic obedience are over. That's what the 1960s meant – no more deference.

Beatlemania
Outside the gates of
Buckingham Palace on
the day the Beatles
received their MBEs.
Roger Jackson,
Central Press,
26 October 1965
Central Press/
Hulton Getty

TREVOR PHILLIPS

Bobby Moore (Captain) with his English team mates celebrating victory in the World Cup Final, Wembley. From left to right: Jack Charlton (born 1935); Nobby Stiles (born 1942); Alan Ball (born 1945); Martin Peters (born 1943); Geoff Hurst (born 1941); Bobby Moore (1941–93); Ray Wilson (born 1934); George Cohen (born 1939); Bobby Charlton (born 1937)
Bippa, 30 July 1966
Popperfoto

NOT ONLY was this really a sublime day – golden sun and all the rest of it – but it marked the moment when the 'people's game', football, officially swept cricket aside. Football had always been the game of working-class boys, but up to this point it had not stood for the national character in the way it does now. The victory, at home, and over the Germans – who else would do as symbolic enemies? – was an affirmation of Britain's confidence, and the right of working-class people to represent the whole nation. Alongside the Beatles, Twiggy, Michael Caine and Harold Wilson, this afternoon buried the tugging of forelocks forever. The theme of 'poor boy made good through sport' was the legacy of the most memorable athlete of the century – Cassius Clay (Muhammad Ali), a Southern boy who came to dominate the world with his fists, his wit and his refusal ever to bow his head to anyone. He defeated Henry Cooper, who was the epitome of the old deference – a working-class lad, who always seemed to believe that he wasn't as good as the 'posh people'.

TREVOR PHILLIPS

Tony Blair (born 1953)
and Peter Mandelson
(born 1953) unveiling a
model of the Millennium
Dome at the Festival Hall.
Brian Harris, 1998
National Portrait Gallery,
London

'WE ARE the masters now.' Not really. A hundred years ago, the monarch and his or her government would have decided how to celebrate the Millennium, and then told the people, who would have had to accept it and meekly trot along and marvel. Not any more. Here the authors of the Dome are having to sell the concept to a sceptical public. The photograph could just as easily depict a company chairman and chief executive presenting a new plan to shareholders. They know that they have borrowed power only for as long as they keep us happy; as indeed the former Trade Secretary Peter Mandelson knows to his cost, a fall can come swiftly. Blair and Mandelson were pilloried for relying on focus groups and polls; but perhaps they were simply the first to realise that governments can no longer ignore the ordinary people between elections, and that life at the top is more precarious than it has ever been. The rulers are now there only because we want them to be there, not because they were born to it. And that's as it should be.

TREVOR PHILLIPS

DAVID PUTTNAM

BORN IN London in 1941, David Puttnam was educated at Minchenden Grammar School before beginning a career as a photographer's agent and advertising executive. In 1968 he entered the film industry. In 1986 he became Chairman and Chief Executive of Columbia Pictures in Hollywood, but returned permanently to Britain in 1988. His feature films, which among them have won every major international award, include *Bugsy Malone* (1976), *Midnight Express* (1978), *Chariots of Fire* (1981), *Local Hero* (1982), *The Killing Fields* (1985), *The Mission* (1986), *Memphis Belle* (1990) and, most recently, *My Life So Far* (1999). He has also produced a number of films and series for television. He received a CBE in 1983, was knighted in 1995, and two years later was appointed to the House of Lords as a Life Peer.

AS THIS troubled century draws to a close, one extraordinary social achievement stands out that would, I believe, have been inconceivable in 1950, let alone 1900. Britain is now, and forever will be, a multi-cultural society – and a reasonably successful one at that.

I think it's fair to say that any serious student of social change who, even up to the end of the Second World War, had the foresight to suggest the possibility of today's multi-faith, multi-ethnic Britain would almost certainly have been regarded as a Utopian fantasist.

Although the transition has been rapid, it has not been easy or untroubled; in fact, it's been an edgy and evolving story, as I hope my selection of ten images manages to convey.

On the face of it, at the turn of the century Britain had quite a lot to shout about. Possessor of the most extensive empire the world had ever known, this relatively small if densely populated island had brought together dozens and dozens of disparate races and nationalities into a coherent and comparatively well-regulated community of nations. Admittedly, not much argument was brooked as to who was 'Mother', but in varying degrees all the peoples of the Empire possessed rights, status and at least the notion of mutual obligation under the Crown.

In these circumstances Britains found themselves reasonably adjusted to the extraordinary diversity of colour, race and creed embraced within their Empire – in fact, many were incredibly proud of it.

This affection for Empire and its later transition into an altogether more sustainable 'Commonwealth' glosses over what in reality became a rather schizophrenic attitude towards multi-culturalism. Few people in Britain in the early part of the century would have believed that the rights of many of the Empire's citizens would come to be exercised here at home, in the mother country.

Yet the past forty years have seen the abandonment of Empire and the emergence of what is, in every respect, a new and very different nation, one that has absorbed its multi-cultural future with a degree of confidence that must have left the early apostles of racial doom almost speechless.

I've mentioned it being an 'edgy' transition, for while we have achieved successes that few would have believed possible, it's equally true that we remain little more than half-way towards the type of relaxed, generous and inclusive society we all dream of being a part of.

DAVID PUTTNAM

WE APPEAL TO GREAT BRITAIN TO STOP THE BUTCHERY OF JEWS IN POLAND

We PROTEST AGAINST
THE CONTINUED SLAUGHTER
OF INNOCENT JEWISH
WOMEN AND CHILDREN
IN POLAND.

THE FIRST significant wave of immigration in the early part of this century was largely made up of Jews from Eastern and Central Europe.

They brought energy and imagination to the East End of London and those other areas such as Manchester, Leeds and Glasgow in which they sought to establish stable and successful communities.

This photograph shows how those who had escaped persecution in their own countries campaigned for freedom for those they'd left behind.

Jewish Protest, East End,
London.
Unknown photographer,
26 June 1919
Topical Press/
Hulton Getty

DAVID PUTTNAM

AS FASCISM spread across Europe, that ever-seductive pawn, anti-Semitism, came into play. In Britain this hate- (or fear-) based movement found its focus in Sir Oswald Mosley and his so-called 'Blackshirts'. It's greatly to the credit of this country's tradition of democratic tolerance that Mosley never emerged as much more than an exotic fringe player on the national scene.

The photographer on the extreme left covering this fascist parade in London in 1936 is my father, Len Puttnam.

Sir Oswald Mosley
(1896–1980) inspecting
members of the British
Union of Fascists in
Royal Mint Street,
London.
Unknown photographer,
October 1936
Central Press/
Hulton Getty

DAVID PUTTNAM

EVEN IN a generally tolerant society
like Britain, nascent fascism lurks fairly
close to the surface.

All that's needed is the truculent
dissatisfaction of an unfulfilled
minority to fuse with the ambitions of
a charismatic or manipulative political
figure, and you have the potential for
crisis.

Edward Heath, in promptly
distancing himself and his party from
Enoch Powell's polemic, saved the
country from the possibility of schism.

Racist Graffiti
Unknown photographer,
1 May 1968
Evening Standard/
Hulton Getty

RACIAL TENSION has erupted on a number of occasions this past century, most notably in Brixton in early 1981.

The disorders were communal disturbances arising from a complex political, social and economic situation, which is not special to Brixton.

Once begun, the disorders on the Friday and the Saturday soon developed into a riot. The common purpose of the riots was to attack the police. But the riots were neither premeditated nor planned. Each was the spontaneous reaction of angry young men, most of whom were black, against what they saw as a hostile police force.

From *The Brixton Disorders*, Report of an Inquiry by the Rt Hon. The Lord Scarman, OBE November 1981

Brixton Riots
John Hodder,
1 January 1981
The *Observer*/
Hulton Getty

DAVID PUTTNAM

Bank Holiday Monday,
Notting Hill Carnival.
Unknown photographer,
27 August 1979
'PA' Photos

STARTING AS an exotic and thoroughly un-British phenomenon, the Notting Hill Carnival quickly established itself as a cultural fixture in the life of the capital.

It's now been successfully transplanted to other British cities, most notably Belfast, where it has taken on an important role as a large and hugely enjoyable festival of art and culture. A reminder, should we ever need it, that multi-culturalism is about much more than race.

Passengers from the
Empire Windrush
Unknown photographer,
June 1948
Popperfoto

BRITAIN HAS a long history of political and, rather more recently, religious tolerance. Political dissidents from all over the world have found a secure and lawful home in this country, never more so than during the inter-war years, when many thousands of refugees from fascist Europe found a safe haven here. But the dominant changes in Britain today were driven by migration from the West Indies in the mid-1950s and by Asians from Africa and the Sub-Continent in the 1960s and 1970s.

It is the descendants of these two groups who have forever changed the face of Britain.

The *Empire Windrush* docked at Tilbury in June 1948. This image captures the hopes and fears of that moment as well as any I've come across.

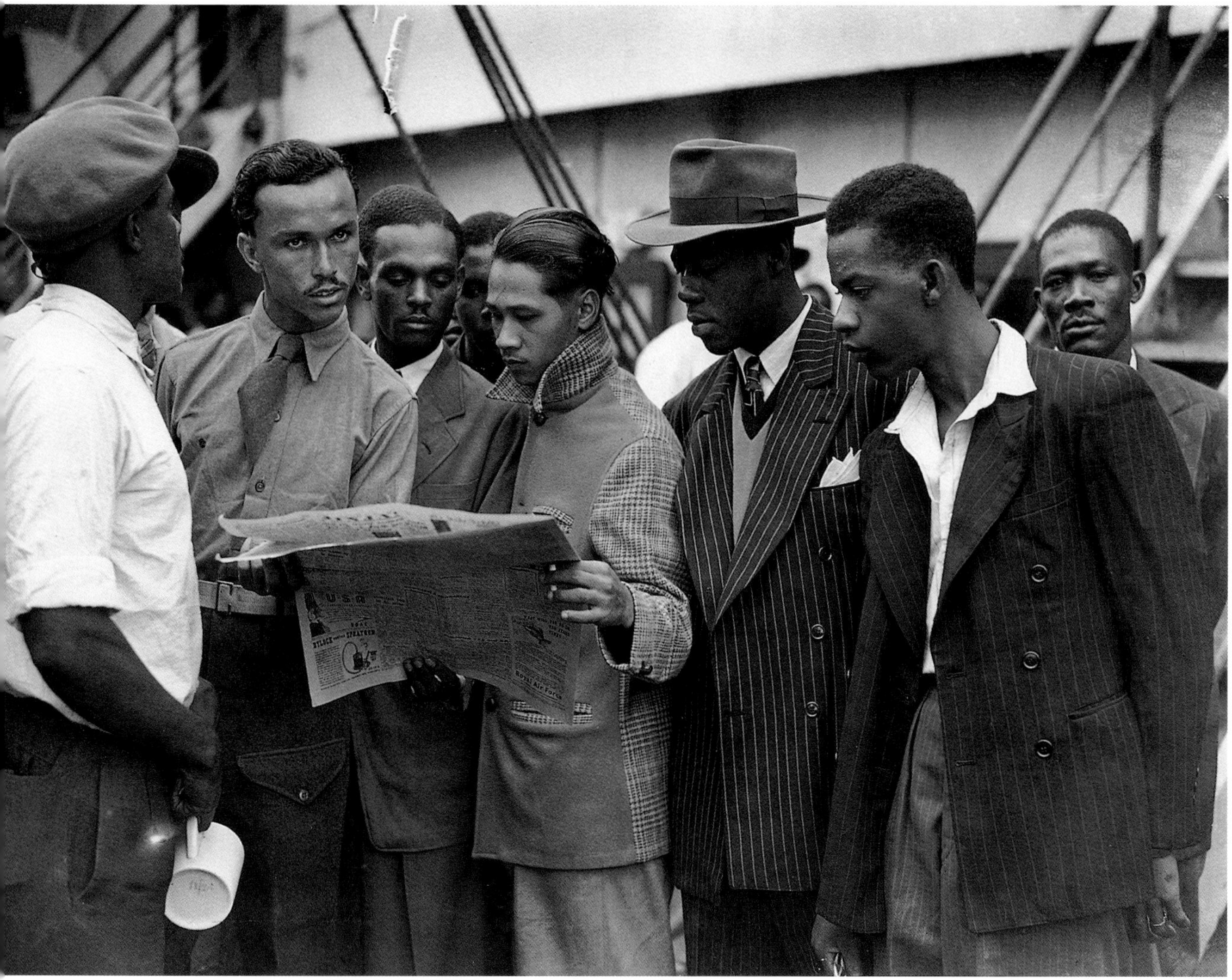

DAVID PUTTNAM

Colin Jackson (born 1967)
Clive Brunskill,
31 July 1997
Clive Brunskill/
Allsport Photographic

THE UNION flag has been used and
abused in defence of any number of
versions (and perversions) of
nationhood during this past 100 years.

As a hopeful and sustainable
image of Britain on the cusp of the
Millennium, I'm not sure that this
image of Colin Jackson, one of the
most elegant and articulate athletes
ever to have represented his country,
can possibly be beaten.

For me, it looks to the future with
a bright and burning confidence.
As a nation we can ask for no more.

DAVID PUTTNAM

THE CULTURAL impact of the Asian community in this country has taken many forms.

Our tastes in food and fashion have been transformed. Colour has entered our lives as never before, and the importance of tradition, education, commitment and family have been powerfully reinforced.

This gathering in London offers an image of Britain in the 1990s that was probably inconceivable even one generation earlier.

THE SOCIAL and commercial courage of the Asian community is one of the great success stories of twentieth-century Britain. Asian businessmen and women literally changed the face and living patterns of a nation.

They opened earlier, closed later, stocked more and charged less, and in doing so became the social focus of communities up and down the country. Their influence now extends well beyond small retail outlets and their longer term impact on Britain's economy has only just begun to be evident.

Punjabi newsagents, Westbourne Park, London.
Crispin Hughes, early 1990s
Crispin Hughes/ Photofusion

DAVID PUTTNAM

BRITAIN'S CHILDREN are growing up in
a country much of which is socially
unrecognisable to their parents, let
alone grandparents. They are the latest
chapter in what started as an organic
cultural experiment but which has
been transformed into the most vital,
energising and hopeful human
phenomenon imaginable.

JOHN SAINSBURY

BORN IN 1927, Lord Sainsbury of Preston Candover was educated at Stowe School and at Worcester College, Oxford, where he was made an honorary fellow in 1982. In 1950 he entered the family business, J. Sainsbury PLC, becoming a Director in 1958. He was appointed Chairman in 1969, retiring in 1992, when he was made Life President. His interests in opera and ballet and the visual arts have led to a number of appointments in these areas: he has served as a trustee of the National Gallery, the Tate Gallery, the Westminster Abbey Trust and Dulwich Picture Gallery, and as Vice-President of the Contemporary Arts Society; he was Director then Chairman of the Royal Opera House, Covent Garden (1987–91), and is Chairman of the Governors of the Royal Ballet. He is also a Director of the Friends of the Nelson Mandela Children's Fund and President of Sparsholt College, Hampshire. He was created a Life Peer, as Baron Sainsbury of Preston Candover, in 1989, and a Knight of the Garter in 1992.

IN CHOOSING my ten Faces of the Century I was anxious that those I selected would not only have contributed significantly to British life this past century but were likely to be remembered and admired in a hundred years' time. I have long believed that, to a far greater extent than in other vocations, it is the work of writers, poets, painters, sculptors and composers that carries on across the centuries to enlighten the experience of successive generations. Their contribution to the quality of life, I believe, can be matched only by that of great scientists. Therefore with one exception I have not chosen any political leaders, because, though of importance in their time, generally they will be barely remembered in a hundred years.

Nine of my ten choices are considerable creative artists of whom our nation can be proud and who have in this century made major contributions in the world of the arts and literature. They are great 'creative' faces not only of this century but for the future, not only for Britain but for many around the world.

JOHN SAINSBURY

THOMAS HARDY was a writer of genius whose novels, written near the end of the nineteenth century, were the most successful and admired fiction in the early years of this century. Among the most famous are *Far from the Madding Crowd* (1874), *The Return of the Native* (1878) and *Tess of the D'Urbervilles* (1891).

In the first quarter of this century Hardy returned to his first love – poetry – and wrote some of the finest poems of our time. He received the Order of Merit in 1910 and, to his great delight, the Freedom of Dorchester!

Thomas Hardy
(1840–1928)
Clive Holland, 1900s
Bromide print,
151 x 111mm
National Portrait Gallery,
London (x17358)

JOHN SAINSBURY

BRITTEN'S FIRST great success, which quickly brought him international recognition, was the opera *Peter Grimes*, first performed in June 1945. A further nine operas followed, including *Albert Herring* (1947), *Billy Budd* (1951), *Gloriana* (for the Coronation in 1953), *The Turn of the Screw* (1954), *A Midsummer Night's Dream* (1960) and *Death in Venice* (1973).

He also composed many songs, song cycles, chamber and orchestral music and diverse works for chorus and orchestra including his *War Requiem*, written for the opening of the new Coventry cathedral in 1961. He has achieved greater fame and admiration world-wide than any other British composer.

The photograph that I have selected was taken at the time he composed *Peter Grimes*, near Aldeburgh, a small town on the Suffolk coast where he lived from 1947 to the end of his life.

Benjamin Britten (1913–76), Snape, Suffolk. Enid Slater, 1944 Bromide print, 164 x 120mm National Portrait Gallery, London (x15200)

JOHN SAINSBURY

T.S. ELIOT, poet, playwright, critic, editor and publisher, was British by adoption. He left the United States in his twenties to spend the rest of his life in England, becoming a British subject in 1927.

I believe he was the contemporary poet of greatest influence on my generation, and I well remember the excitement of meeting him when at Oxford and the reverence in which we held his famous poem *The Waste Land* (1922). He described it as 'just a piece of rhythmical grumbling', but, in the words of Richard Ellman, 'it broke with traditional structure . . . and with all its mustering of past ages, it spoke sharply to its own time'. *The Hollow Men* (1925) and *Four Quartets* (1944) were also widely and deservedly admired.

His plays *Murder in the Cathedral* (1935) and *The Cocktail Party* (1950) contained great writing and enjoyed huge success. His most unexpected theatrical contribution, however, must be his collection of poems written in 1939, *Old Possum's Book of Practical Cats*, which formed the basis of the musical *Cats*.

T.S. (Thomas Stearns)
Eliot (1888–1965)
Kay Bell Reynal, 1955
Bromide print,
340 x 267mm
National Portrait Gallery,
London (P205)

JOHN SAINSBURY

HENRY MOORE was the sculptor of the century with, for me, a real touch of genius. I will always cherish the memory of visiting his studio in 1969 when my wife and I enjoyed his warm and generous hospitality. While we admired his current work, both huge pieces sited in a distant field and small maquettes in the studio, he enthused about the beauty of the head of our three-month-old babe.

Henry Moore (1898–1986)
Ida Kar, 1954
Bromide print,
197 × 205mm
National Portrait Gallery,
London (x13791)

JOHN SAINSBURY

ELGAR'S MARVELLOUS *Variations on an
Original Theme* ('Enigma Variations')
was composed in 1899 and from that
point his genius was increasingly
widely recognised. It was followed by
the oratorio *Dream of Gerontius* (1900)
and a period of great creative energy
that lasted until 1920. He was a
symphonic writer on an epic scale, the
composer of the hymn 'Land of Hope
and Glory' as well as of concertos of
great sensitivity. *Enigma Variations* was
used by Frederick Ashton for a
marvellous ballet first performed
in 1968.

Richard Strauss described 'Meister
Elgar' as the first English progressive
musician. Much honoured in his
lifetime, Elgar was the first musician to
be awarded the Order of Merit, an
honour richly deserved for the man
who did so much to raise the status of
English music.

Sir Edward Elgar
(1857–1934)
E.T. Holding, 1905
Platinum print,
193 x 109mm
National Portrait Gallery,
London (x11905)

JOHN SAINSBURY

WITHOUT DOUBT Churchill was our greatest statesman of the century and the greatest wartime leader of the nation in its most desperate hour of need.

He contributed more to the defeat of fascism than any other western leader, and undoubtedly had greater impact on those who heard his wartime speeches, as I did, and 'witnessed' his leadership, than any other of our political leaders.

He was a master of the English language, a marvellous writer and a distinguished historian. That great understanding and knowledge of history gave his statesmanship a dimension largely absent among today's politicians.

For me, if there could be one Face of the Century it should be Winston Churchill.

The Rt. Hon. Winston
Churchill (1874–1965)
Robert Elliot, 1943
Vintage print,
252 x 202mm
National Portrait Gallery,
London (x17071)

JOHN SAINSBURY

Noël Coward (1899–1973)
Dorothy Wilding, 1951
Vintage print,
296 x 207mm
National Portrait Gallery,
London (x6929)

NOËL COWARD was the Congreve of our day, according to Arnold Bennett writing in 1930, at the time that *Private Lives* was first performed. Coward was the author of many plays including *The Vortex*, which in 1924 was his first great success, and *Blithe Spirit* (1941), his longest running comedy. But apart from being a highly successful playwright, he was a great performer in his plays, in musical comedies, in cabaret and in films (notably *In Which We Serve*, in 1942). Having once heard him singing his own brilliantly composed and witty songs at the Café de Paris in the 1950s, I thought that this photograph shows us the 'elegant entertainer' with all the flair and humour that imbued his theatrical life and made him the epitome of those times.

JOHN SAINSBURY

SIR KENNETH MacMillan was the brilliant Royal Ballet choreographer who created what have become the second generation of great classical ballets.

His *Romeo and Juliet* (1965), *Manon* (1974) and *Mayerling* (1978) in a very different, but nevertheless real sense, are as important in the repertory of ballet as are *Sleeping Beauty* and *Swan Lake*. His great one-act ballets *Invitation* (1960), *Rite of Spring* (1962), *Song of the Earth* (1965), *Elite Syncopations* (1974), *Requiem* (1976), *Gloria* (1980) and *The Judas Tree* (1992) extend the boundary of dance, having great contemporary relevance and humanity and a timeless emotional quality.

Sir Kenneth MacMillan
(1929–92)
Julian Broad,
September 1992
Bromide fibre print,
274 x 394mm
National Portrait Gallery

Francis Bacon (1909–92)
Barry Joule, 1982
Barry Joule

BORN IN Ireland, Francis Bacon was the century's greatest British painter, recognised and admired throughout the world, and whose work I believe future generations will value more than that of any of today's British artists. He was a self-taught artist who deliberately subverted artistic conventions, creating disturbing human forms that are powerful and unsettling images.

JOHN SAINSBURY

209

THE FOUNDER and creator of the Royal Ballet, Dame Ninette de Valois has done more than anyone for British dance. With single-minded dedication, she built up a ballet company (originally the Vic-Wells, then Sadler's Wells before becoming the Royal Ballet in 1956) from small beginnings to the great company whose performance of *Sleeping Beauty* so triumphantly reopened the Royal Opera House in 1946. It has since been one of the world's leading classical ballet companies, led for many years by Margot Fonteyn, but with a great wealth of talent at all levels.

The founder also of the Royal Ballet School, she was a great visionary who was both loved and feared by dancers – she had a fiery Irish temperament – and respected and admired by all with a love of dance. Like Diaghilev, she drew on the finest talent of the day, whether composers, artist/designers or choreographers.

She was once a dancer herself, first performing, like Noël Coward, on the stage at the age of fourteen, as one of the 'Wonder Children' who toured pier theatres in 1913–14. As a choreographer she created some outstanding ballets, notably *Job* (1931), *Rakes Progress* (1935) and *Checkmate* (1937). She was also a brilliant speaker, and an outstanding writer of prose and poetry.

Dame Ninette de Valois
(born 1898)
Gordon Anthony, 1937
Bromide fibre print,
493 × 377mm
National Portrait Gallery,
London (x44790)

JOHN SAINSBURY

VIVIENNE WESTWOOD

BORN IN Derbyshire in 1941, Vivienne Westwood moved to London when she was 17. Her first career was as a primary school teacher. She began to design fashion in 1970 in partnership with the rock-music entrepreneur Malcolm McLaren. During their time of collaboration, they created the 'Punk' look and then the Pirate and Buffalo collections. In 1984 Westwood launched the 'mini-crini', a version of the Victorian crinoline. The feminine and sexy clothes for which she is now best known were exaggerated to an extreme in the collection 'Vive La Cocotte' in 1995. In 1992 she was awarded an OBE, and in 1998 the Queen's Award for Export.

I CHOSE the photographs with some sense of responsibility of what people might expect of me – photographs that focus on fashion, which have entered the public domain and which are of personal interest; yet because I define myself by what I think, the really profound influences on my life have been in a larger sphere, so I gave an intimation of this by choosing Bertrand Russell, the greatest thinker of our century, and placing him as the final portrait, though according to the date of the photograph he should have been placed second.

I wanted to have a photograph of a lady in a Worth gown because it is a great treasure that so much of Worth's work was photographed, and I remembered seeing in one of my books' the splendid gown he created for Lady Curzon. Since its invention the camera has helped to define beauty, and the long exposure required in early photography presented the sitter as composed and still with soft shaded features and bone structure, an effect that was probably repeated in the evenings of gas light, or the daytimes shaded by hats, parasols and veils.

VIVIENNE WESTWOOD

This early choice determined a selection through the intervening years up to the present.

Each of the subjects is a glamorous icon, a person who stood for something so special that it would not exist without them. Looking at the line-up, it is striking how great a part clothes play in communicating that presence, and it is striking also to see how the style of each photographer has caught the individual at a point in time each so different: the styling and photographic mood of the picture of Vivien Leigh is very Hollywood, though she herself is so aloof, intelligent, lonely and alone; Elizabeth II, whose glamour depends entirely on the belief in her by her subjects, is photographed by the incomparable Beaton in an age that will never return; Elizabeth Taylor caught by the camera flash belongs to an age when the night of the Oscars was really a night of stars who endured; Jean Shrimpton modelled in an age when clothes and accessories did something for you – men whistled at you in the streets; Johnny Rotten, dark, graphic and black photographed against a white background, a hero for youth who tried and failed to rock the establishment – all rock 'n roll has to be token rebellion after that; Sara Stockbridge, my 'mini-crini girl', has gone her own sweet way and if ever young kids should try to recreate her look it would be like a soulless cliché; Margaret Thatcher (impersonated by me), the ultimate in 1980s power dressing, the perfect casting for a horror film – though she has gone her values represent everything that is horrifying in the world; Helena Bonham Carter, looking rather worried, at the end of the 1990s; and Bertrand Russell who sees the future.

VIVIENNE WESTWOOD

MARY LEITER was an American beauty. One of the rich heiresses who married into the English aristocracy, she became Lady Curzon. As the Vicereine of India she commissioned the sumptuous fabric of her dress from Indian craftsmen, to be embroidered in a peacock design, the eyes of which were made from blue and green iridescent beetle wings. The gown was executed by Worth. She wears all her jewellery at once, to vie with the Indian princes.

Mary, Viscountess
Curzon, Vicereine of
India (1870–1906), India
Jeakins, 1902
Museum of London

VIVIENNE WESTWOOD

Vivien Leigh (1913–67)
as Lady Hamilton in
That Hamilton Woman.
Laszlo Willinger, 1941
The John Kobal
Foundation

VIVIEN LEIGH was my mother's film heroine and I was named after her. I agree with my mother that I have never seen a prettier woman. Sitting alone in her big bed with her totally Hollywood, Greek-draped nightie, she maintains her English aloofness.

VIVIENNE WESTWOOD

THE PARAPHERNALIA and pose for the
official Coronation portrait are in
a line of tradition continued from
painting. The dress by Norman
Hartnell is embroidered with the floral
emblems of the British Isles and
complements the importance of the
royal regalia with its stunning jewels.
Cecil Beaton has captured the Queen's
expression of commitment, and her
red lips are at the centre of the
composition.

Her Majesty Queen
Elizabeth II (born 1926)
in her Coronation robes.
Cecil Beaton, 2 June 1953
Semi-matt cibachrome,
331 x 249mm
National Portrait Gallery,
London (x35390)

VIVIENNE WESTWOOD

Elizabeth Taylor (born
1932) and Richard Burton
(1925–84) at the 42nd
Academy Awards
ceremony, Los Angeles.
Richard M. Hudson,
7 April 1970
The Academy of Motion
Picture Arts & Sciences

ELIZABETH TAYLOR radiates the joy of
living; I think that she and her
husband may have come in from the
sun (perhaps after one of the famous
Burton-Taylor rows) and then enjoyed
themselves dressing up for the Oscar
party: she had her raven hair dressed
and applied matching shadow above
her violet-blue eyes, anticipating the
colour of her designer dress, which has
a strong foundation to hold her in but
lets it appear that the bodice is a mere
scrap of mousseline that can hardly
contain her bursting breasts; the
necklace is a triumph of irony and
bravura.

JEAN SHRIMPTON was outstandingly photogenic; she must have been one of the most photographed icons of the 1960s. She is wearing the famous 'page boy' look of Yves Saint-Laurent.

Jean Shrimpton (born 1943)
wearing Yves Saint-Laurent
Guy Bourdin, 1965
Courtesy Schirmer/Mosel,
Munich

VIVIENNE WESTWOOD

Johnny Rotten (John
Lydon; born 1956)
Ray Stevenson, 1976
Vivienne Westwood

THIS IS the best portrait of a punk:
Johnny Rotten, Urban Guerrilla; the
ultimate fantasy of youth. The original
photograph is lost but we have a copy
of the one that sports the graffiti
Johnny Rotten scrawled on it. The
bondage suit is by Westwood/McLaren.

Handsome
John Rotten L.T.D.

A TRUE STAR OF OUR TIMES MAAAN!

A SEX PISTOLS HERO

Sara Stockbridge
Nick Knight, 1987
Nick Knight

SARA STOCKBRIDGE with her long limbs walks like a naughty doll, and her presence on the catwalk was one of superb auto-irony. Here she is winking for the cover of *I.D.*, wearing my Harris Tweed crown and fake ermine tippet. I styled her platinum hair in big pin curls, keeping in the clips that achieved for me the look of an eighteenth-century wig. Nick Knight's photography bears his unmistakable chic.

VIVIENNE WESTWOOD

HERE I am impersonating Margaret Thatcher. It is a testimony as to how I estimated the hypocrisy of the woman. The photograph was on the cover of *Tatler* and bore the sub-title 'This woman was once a Punk'. Aquascutum were very cross at the use we made of the suit she ordered, which she then cancelled.

Vivienne Westwood (born 1941) as Margaret Thatcher. Michael Roberts, April 1988 Michael Roberts/ Maconochie Photography

DAVID SEIDNER was the only photographer that I ever met who adored couture gowns enough to examine them in museum archives. He chose one of my most extravagant gowns to show off Helena's beautiful décolleté and her nearly white, tissue-fine complexion. She is an English rose.

Helena Bonham Carter
(born 1966)
David Seidner, 1998
Colour print,
604 x 498mm
National Portrait Gallery,
London

VIVIENNE WESTWOOD

I HAVE chosen nine photographs that focus on fashion, but for me real glamour starts here (he does look like the Mad Hatter) with this portrait of Bertrand Russell. The quality of his thinking changed my life forever. A full-face portrait from this sitting reveals the infinite curiosity and profound knowledge of his beautiful eyes, but I have chosen the profile because the way that the light strikes his head says 'philosopher'.

Bertrand Russell, 3rd Earl Russell (1872–1970) Howard Coster, 1935 National Portrait Gallery, London (x14658)

VIVIENNE WESTWOOD

237

Picture Credits

© Frank Ockenfels 3: p.14; © Jane Bown: pp.16–17, 34, 54, 74, 98, 118, 140, 164, 190 and 214; © Frank Thurston: p.18; © Hulton Getty: pp.20, 21, 24, 51, 60–61, 62, 78, 82, 90–91, 124–5, 128–9, 131, 152–3, 155, frontispiece (detail) and 156–8, 168–9, 170–71, 172–3, 174–5; © Reserved James Scott: pp.22–3; © Steve Speller: p.25; © Bob Gruen: p.27; © Reserved. Reproduced courtesy of the Mander and Mitchenson Theatre Collection: pp.28–9; © Snowdon: pp.31, 95, 115; © Bolton Museum and Art Gallery: p.38; Courtesy of the Museum of London: pp.40, 57, 121, 218; © Stuart Franklin/Magnum Photos: pp.42–3; © Michael Joseph: p.44; © Martin Jenkinson: p.47; © Jim Barron: p.48; © Stephen Shakeshaft: p.49; © Popperfoto: pp.50, 158–9, 178–9; Trustees of the Imperial War Museum: pp.58–9, 89, 122–3, 126; © London Transport Museum: p.63; © David Bailey: p.64; © Susan Greenhill: pp.66–7; © David Buckland: p.68; © National Portrait Gallery/image courtesy of Camera Press: p.69; © John Giles/'PA' Photos: pp.70–71; © Topham Picture Point: pp.77, 148; Courtesy of Auberon Waugh: pp.80–81; Reproduced courtesy of Lord Tweedsmuir: p.85; Still reproduced by permission of Carlton International Media Ltd: p.86; Courtesy of Sotheby's London: p.92; © Antony Barrington Brown: pp.100–01; Reproduced courtesy of DAMTP, The University of Cambridge: p.103;

© Norman Parkinson. Courtesy of Hamiltons: p.104; © Reserved: p.107, 193, 198, 201, 202; © Reserved, image courtesy of UKAEA, pp.110–11; Courtesy of Alexander Fleming Laboratory Museum and St Mary's Hospital Medical School Audiovisual Services: p.112; © Mirror Syndication International: p.130; © John Walmsley: p.132; © Neil Libbert: pp.134–5; © Colin Edwards/Photofusion: p.137; © Trustees of the Broadlands Archives: pp.146–7; © Koo Stark/Stark-Image: p.149; © Freud Museum, London: p.150; © The *Independent*: p.160; © 'PA' Photos: p.177; © Allsport/Clive Brunskill: pp.180–81; © Judy Goldhill: p.183; © Crispin Hughes/Photofusion: p.184; © Joanne O'Brien/Format: p.187; © Estate of Enid Slater: p.194; © Kay Bell Reynal: p.196; © By courtesy of Tom Hustler/National Portrait Gallery, London: p.205; © Julian Broad: pp.206–7; © Barry Joule: pp.208–9; © Theatre Museum: p.211; Print courtesy of The John Kobal Foundation: p.221; Courtesy of the Victoria and Albert Museum: p.222; Photograph © The Academy of Motion Pictures Arts & Sciences: p.225; © Guy Bourdin: p.226; © Ray Stevenson: p.229; © Nick Knight: p.230; © Michael Roberts: p.233; © David Seidner: p.234.

Index